JOHN LISTON
COMEDIAN

by
JIM DAVIS

THE SOCIETY FOR THEATRE RESEARCH

First published 1985
by The Society for Theatre Research
77 Kinnerton Street, London SW1X 8ED

ISBN 0 85430 039 2

Printed in Great Britain at
The Bath Press, Avon

Foreword

Among the great English players of the first third of the nineteenth century, perhaps the least well known now is John Liston; and yet in his day his popularity was enormous and his reputation stood high. As Paul Pry his catch-phrase – "Hope I dont intrude?" entered the language in the 1820s as Mrs. Mopp's "Can I do yer now, sir?" did in the 1940s. Yet until now there has been no full-length biography of him available.

That he was primarily a comedian in the days of the great Romantic tragedians – Kemble, Cooke, Kean – may be part of the explanation; yet so were Munden and Grimaldi, and they are still popularly remembered; but Charles Lamb wrote immortally about Munden, and Hazlitt and Leigh Hunt about Grimaldi, and both players left their own memoirs, which were edited and published in the years after their deaths. These were powerful memorials. Liston had neither.

Jim Davis has set out to remedy this omission, to provide a well-researched and authoritative account of Liston's life, and to attempt to get at the origins and characteristics of his art. In this respect the Liston iconography is particularly abundant, though not easily available. Dr. Davis has assembled a wide collection of illustrations, of which the Society for Theatre Research has decided to include as many as possible, as important evidence. The Society is especially grateful to all those who have helped to provide the necessary prints and photographs.

Arnold Hare
(Editor for The Society for Theatre Research)

Acknowledgements

My first thanks must go, inevitably, to Professor Peter Thomson of Exeter University. It was he who first suggested to me that John Liston might be a fruitful topic to research and it is largely due to his inspiration and encouragement that this study has evolved. Equally, I would like to thank Mrs. Robin Craven of New York. I have enjoyed her friendship from an early stage in my research and she has kindly shared her knowledge with me and provided me with access to her unparalleled collection of Liston iconography. Generously, she has made available photographs of a number of items in her collection as illustrations for this book. My debt to both is enormous.

A number of individuals have been particularly helpful. Gilbert B. Cross and Professor A. L. Nelson kindly provided me with a transcript of relevant material from the Winston Diaries, prior to their publication, and also helped decipher passages outside the years covered in their volume. Clifford J. Williams answered a number of queries for me, as did Professor Appleton.

I would also like to express my thanks for help received to the staffs of the following libraries: the British Library, the Theatre Museum, the Garrick Club Library, the Bodleian Library, the Library of the Victoria and Albert Museum, the Newcastle Central Library, the Harvard Theatre Collection, the New York Public Library Theatre Collection at the Lincoln Centre and the William Seymour Theatre Collection, Princeton University. The following libraries and institutions have kindly answered queries and provided information: Butler Library, University of Columbia; Dorset County Museum; Dublin Public Library; Durham County Library; University Library, Durham; Exeter City Library; the Folger Shakespeare Library, Washington D.C.; the Borough of Gosport Central Public Library; the Greater London Record Office; the Brynmor Jones Library, University of Hull; the Henry E. Huntington Library, San Marino; Manchester Central Library; the National Library of Ireland; the National

Library of Scotland; the North Devon Athenaeum, Barnstaple; Plymouth Central Library; Royal Irish Academy; the Shakespeare Centre, Stratford-upon-Avon; Taunton Public Library; the Archives Department of the City of Westminster Library; the Borough of Weymouth and Melcombe Regis Public Library; York City Library; the Hoblitzelle Theatre Collection, University of Texas.

I am grateful to Dr. Arnold Hare, who has proved a patient and painstaking editor of this volume and has made a number of very helpful suggestions. I should also like to thank John Pemberton for his excellent work in photographing Liston prints from my own collection; Jane Rogers for help with photographs; and all those friends and relatives who have had to live with John Liston for nearly as long as I have.

Within the body of the text I have included a number of anecdotes which were related of Liston during and after his life-time. Anecdotes are, of course, notoriously unreliable. Yet, even when they are not verifiable, they often contain truths about their subjects which are not always accessible in more legitimate sources. The anecdotes that were told about Liston tell us something about how his contemporaries perceived this very private man. Consequently, I feel that no apology is needed for their inclusion, although occasionally they should be taken with a pinch of salt.

London, 1985   *Jim Davis*

Contents

Illustrations

ix

Photography:

Mrs. Robin Craven 3, 8, 16a, 16b, 18, 19, 20, 21, 28a, 28b, 29a, 29b,
30a, 30b, 31a, 31b, 32

Ms. J. E. C. Rogers 7

John David Pemberton 1, 2a, 2b, 2c, 2d, 4a, 4b, 5a, 5b, 6, 9, 10, 11,
12, 17, 21, 22, 23, 24, 25, 26, 27

"Mr Liston is the greatest comic genius of the age".

WILLIAM HAZLITT – 1817

"The actually modern stage, that of 1825, has its own comic wonder, Liston".

JAMES BOADEN – 1825

"Vestris and Kean are the most attractive, except my favourite Liston, and he keeps his ground against any of them".

JOHN BANNISTER – 1828

"Liston is the great popular favourite of the day; he is the only person, with the exception of Mr. Kean who, to use a technical phrase, draws single-handed".

THE ATHENAEUM – 1828

"Of all the actors I have ever seen, Kean and Liston appear to me to be the greatest, and to have the least in common with others of their species. Of the two, perhaps, Liston is the most original".

THE NEW YORK MIRROR – 1830

"Don't tell me that tragic Kean's acting is clever,
For me jolly Liston's the actor for ever".

ANONYMOUS VERSE

Chapter I

Early Life – 1776–1805

As they walked along Charing Cross Rd, up Bow Street, across Drury Lane, or alighted from their carriages in the vicinity of Covent Garden, London theatregoers were full of excitement. Liston, their favourite actor, was coming out in a new role. However bad the play, however inane the part, there was little doubt about Liston's ability to please. More than Kean, more than Vestris, more than any other actor, he could pull in the audiences. The hope of another Van Dunder, Lubin Log, Tristram Sappy, Paul Pry, to add to the gallery of grotesques he portrayed, lured the audiences onwards. His oily, mantling face, his dilated nostrils, "goggle" eyes and carp-like mouth threw them into fits of laughter and rapturous applause as soon as he appeared. The detailed observation of his performance, attention to costume, wigs and props, the originality of each new creation, made them love him even more. Whenever they looked in the windows of print shops and pottery warehouses, likenesses of Liston stared back at them. The fashion for this actor, soon to command a salary higher than any living tragedian, knew no bounds. For, by the mid-1820s, when Liston had achieved the peak of popularity described here, the public was infatuated with him.

In private life Liston was totally unlike the characters he played on stage. However bumptious, vacant or uncouth the vulgar cockneys he impersonated, his manners privately were those of a gentleman and he mixed in the best social circles. He dressed with great elegance, almost ostentatiously; there was something of the Regency dandy about him. Affluent, happily married, acquainted with many of the leading literary figures and artists of the day, he was a favourite with royalty and a familiar figure in the fashionable quarters of London and Brighton. His life was exemplary and devoid of scandal. He left no memoirs and his letters provide little insight into his personality. His correspondence largely concerns business arrangements, ill health and dinner invitations, couched usually in polite or formal language.

Inclined to melancholy, fond of serious reading, John Liston was nevertheless one of the greatest comic actors England has ever seen. He was celebrated in prints and porcelain more than any other English actor before or since. He was acclaimed by such critics and men of letters as Hazlitt, Leigh Hunt, Lamb and Crabb Robinson. The newspapers and journals of the early nineteenth century were full of reports which testified to his ability to hold together any comedy, farce or melodrama, however mediocre in the writing. He was a means of bringing people together. Hazlitt, considering the difficulties of communicating with strangers, with whom one has nothing in common, concluded:

> But if he has fortunately ever seen Mr Liston act, this is an immediate topic of mutual conversation, and we agree together the rest of the evening in discussing the merits of that inimitable actor, with the same satisfaction as talking over the affairs of the most intimate friend.

For over thirty years Liston appeared regularly in London's major theatres as well as making frequent excursions into the provinces. In a succession of ephemeral plays he created a long line of original characters and experienced a rapport with his audience enjoyed by very few actors. By night the aloof, pensive man transformed himself into his absurd, awkward characters and brought forth unrequited laughter. The enigma of this metamorphosis from private man to public actor, the effortlessness with which he performed his characters on stage, the industry and art that went into his impersonations, are all worthy of consideration. This biography is an attempt to record the life and work of a man whose contribution to the early nineteenth century English stage was comparable to that of Kemble, Kean, Macready, Grimaldi and Madame Vestris. In his own time he was the embodiment of low comedy and one of the most valuable properties in the theatrical market-place.

John Liston was born in 1776. Throughout his life he preferred to draw a veil over his origins, so that little is known of his family background. His father reputedly lived in Norris Street in the parish of St. James's, but Liston's birth is not recorded in the parish registers. Nor is his birth recorded in the parish registers of St. Ann's, Soho, which several memoirs assign as his place of birth. His father was a cook's shop keeper, who acted as a sutler to some of the inferior gambling houses in Westminster. It was customary, in these houses, to place a supply of ham and beef on the sideboards to display the munificence of the proprietors and to recruit the strength of exhausted players. Liston's father, so one memoir tells us, was well known in sporting circles. He was a man "of very eccentric habits, and more eccentric sayings, but, from his devotion to the gaming table, became reduced".[1] He had a strong sense of humour and his conversation was extremely entertaining, but his improvidence left him employed in a very lowly position in the custom-house. His son, apparently, refused to acknowledge his father in later life and an angry series of letters passed between them in the newspapers.

In fact, Liston's father cannot have been too poor initially, for he managed to send his son to Soho Academy, a respectable school situated in Soho Square, much frequented by the sons of prosperous tradesmen in the district. When the young Liston attended the school, it was under the control of Dr. William Barrow, who had recently been appointed Headmaster. Soho Academy had an outstanding reputation for private performances of plays and its ex-pupils included the actors John Fawcett, John Bannister and Joseph Holman, and the playwright Thomas Morton. Dr. Barrow had changed all that: the youth of the time, he considered, were far too forward to require the liberating influence of public performance. Play acting impaired discipline, inflamed the emotions and filled the heads of the pupils with the most unworthy ambitions. If Liston had hoped to participate in Soho Academy's famous performances, he must have been disappointed by Barrow's decision to discontinue the practice.[2]

Even though he was deprived of dramatic activity at school, Liston could always visit the patent theatres, so long as he could raise a sixpence for half-price or a shilling for the gallery. Sometimes, if he was lucky, he might even procure an order for free admission to one of the theatres. During the winter months he could watch the plays of Shakespeare or Sheridan, at Drury Lane or Covent Garden, and delight in the acting of John Philip Kemble, Sarah Siddons, Joseph Holman and many others. In the summer, when the little theatre in the Haymarket opened its doors, he could indulge in its annual banquet of comedy and farce. He was, it was generally believed, a great enthusiast for tragedy and longed to be a tragic actor. But at least one witness recalled that he was much enamoured by the eccentric movements and diction of Joseph Munden, then England's leading comic actor, and that nothing could keep him out of the theatre when Munden was performing.

By the time he was in his late teens Liston was a source of worry to his father. Fearing that his son's propensity for mischief might lead him into loose habits, the elder Liston secured him the post of usher, or assistant master, at the Library School, in Castle Street. He was employed by the ferocious William Pownall, whose major gratification seemed to be flagellation. "Let this little gentleman feel the rod!" was a regular cry of this awe-inspiring man. Trouble was always brewing and punishments were meted out frequently. The pupils were a noisy, obstreperous, ragged crowd, sent there by their parents to keep them out of mischief during the day. Pownall and Liston, whose salary was £30 a year, had the most profound contempt for each other and the boys were not long in discerning their mutual hatred. Matters came to a head one Easter, when Liston decided to put on a play with the boys he taught. Pownall was away and Liston encouraged the boys to rehearse and to paint some scenery for the play, *Tipoo Sahib*, which was written by Macfarren, one of his pupils. Eventually the play was presented to an audience, who paid twopence at the door for admission. On the third night of the performance Pownall returned home unexpectedly. He was so incensed at the great noise coming from the school room that he went down and poked his head through a window to see what was going on. In mid-performance he publicly reprimanded Liston and told the audience that, if they did not disperse immediately, he would call for aid. Liston he instantly dismissed. If the report of one ex-pupil is to be believed, Liston had had a few drinks when the altercation took place and the two men came to blows. The pupils joined in, Liston and Pownall rolled over onto the floor, and slates, inkstands, rules and forms were used as weapons. So fierce was the combat, the parish beadle and his assistants were called in to appease the fray and the school was eventually closed down for a short time.[3]

Whatever the truth of the matter, Liston suddenly found himself without a job. He may have found alternative employment, possibly as a clerk, possibly as a supercargo responsible for selling the goods aboard a merchant ship, but it was the life of an actor that held out most attractions for him. He lived within easy reach of the Drury Lane and Covent Garden theatres and the Haymarket Theatre had been just around the corner from the Castle Street School. In the taverns and coffee-houses in the area he had become acquainted with singers, dancers and actors, especially those attached to the Haymarket. It was through this connection that, on the 15 August, 1799, he made his first professional appearance at a London theatre, playing Rawbold in George Colman the younger's *The Iron Chest*, for Charles Kemble's benefit,[4] and repeated the part three more times. It was an inauspicious beginning, but his career as an actor had commenced.

Liston's family were opposed to his decision to become an actor and refused him financial assistance. Eventually, he obtained help from another source and fitted himself out with the collection of wigs, costumes and props which actors were then expected to supply. After writing for engagements, he was summoned to the Dublin Theatre, for the 1799–1800 season. He made little impact there – not surprisingly, for he was limited to parts like that of Third Soldier in *Bluebeard*[5] – and by the Spring of 1800 he had returned to England. He was next engaged at the Taunton Theatre, where he made his debut on 28 April as Old Norval in Home's *Douglas*. He did not stay long in this company, managed by the eccentric Henry Lee.

By the summer he was in the company assembled to perform at Weymouth whilst George III was in residence. Liston supported leading actors like Quick and Bannister, who were engaged for part of the season to entertain their monarch. He specialised in the "heavy" business: middle-aged murderers, oppressors of the young and virtuous, respectable fathers and old men. His failure in the comic role of Lord Duberly in Colman's *The Heir at Law* convinced him that he lacked comic talent: he saw himself as, potentially, a tragic actor, a view endorsed by the manager. When he chose Launcelot Gobbo for his benefit at the Weymouth Theatre, the manager was most indignant:

> See – he said – the folly of that young man! Every actor has the right to make a fool of himself once in a season, and they are all but too apt to select their benefits as the favourable opportunity for letting the public know it; and thus you have Liston, who is a sterling tragic actor, in the mere hope of attracting a few fools to laugh at him, cares not how great a fool he makes of himself![6]

When the company left Weymouth and moved on to Exeter, Liston was re-engaged, for he appeared regularly in Exeter from February to April, 1801, in a wide range of parts, which even included the Ghost in *Hamlet*. His benefit took place on April 10, after which he began to look around for another engagement. The extreme South West was not the most suitable place to be if you wanted to advance your career as an actor: the best provincial companies were at Bath, York and Newcastle and it was to one of these that Liston now turned his attention. According to Ann Mathews, a close family friend in later years, Liston wrote to Stephen Kemble, manager of the Newcastle circuit, requesting an engagement as a tragedian. Liston's letter arrived just after a dispute had occurred between Kemble and two of his leading tragedians, Egerton and Bew. (Bew later became famous as a prominent Brighton dentist). As Kemble was in considerable difficulty he wrote to Liston and requested him to hasten to Durham, where he needed an actor to play with his sister, Mrs. Siddons, for a number of nights.[7]

In those days it was easier to travel by sea than by land, so Liston immediately boarded a collier to Newcastle, spending his last few shillings on the journey. Not long after the boat had left the Thames estuary a storm arose at sea. The boat was delayed for several days and Liston had to starve, for he did not have enough money with him to purchase extra provisions. Somewhat the worse for wear he eventually disembarked at Newcastle and hastened across country to Durham. Stephen Kemble received him coolly: he had made up his differences with Egerton and Bew and told Liston he was not interested in employing somebody who could not arrive punctually for an engagement. Liston was crestfallen: he was in desperate financial straits and begged Kemble to take him on. This Kemble grudgingly agreed to do, telling him to bide his time until a suitable role was available.

Eventually, so Ann Mathews tells us, Liston made his debut at Durham as Baron Wildenheim, a heavy middle-aged nobleman, in *Lovers' Vows*, an adaptation by Mrs. Inchbald of one of Kotzebue's plays. In order to make a strong impression in the part Liston selected a wig of long, flowing, grey curls, which he thought looked very becoming. The wig, together with a badly fitting costume, provoked a few titters when Liston made his debut, but little acclaim. As he was at a dinner engagement that evening Stephen Kemble commissioned his daughter, Fanny, to watch Liston. "Mr Liston", she reported back to her father, "is a very young man; but he has some good tones in his voice and he speaks very sensibly. I don't think he is a *handsome* man, but perhaps the very extraordinary *wig* he wore, and the manner in which he marked his face, might cause him to appear otherwise".[8]

Once Mrs. Siddons had arrived in Durham extra performers were needed and Liston's services were required once again. He took great offence at the first rehearsal of *The Gamester,* in which he was to play the worthy Jarvis, because Mrs Siddons seemed to be laughing at his appearance and later reprimanded him in a tone of ridicule. She instructed him that, in her last scene, he must forcibly restrain her, to prevent her running after her dead husband. Inwardly determined on revenge Liston decided not to restrain her during the performance, so that the whole effect would look ridiculous. The performance commenced, but when the moment of revenge arrived, Liston impulsively held her back, because he was so moved by her acting. Mrs Siddons later complimented him for his help at a crucial point in the scene.

Liston's next role was Las Casas in Sheridan's *Pizarro*, a role that he had previously played at Taunton. Liston felt that he could do something with this part, hoping to make an impression on Mrs. Siddons and the whole company. On the night of the performance he again donned his wig of flowing curls and put on an ostentatious costume, then walked into the green-room. He excited glances, but no comment, from Kemble and Mrs. Siddons. During the play Mrs Siddons was seated in majesty on a couch at the back of the stage, when Liston entered, supposedly meek and deferential. Unfortunately, he caught his foot on a piece of wood that was jutting out from the scenery and ungracefully jerked forward, so that he fell sprawling in front of Pizarro on his hands and knees. His white costume was dirtied, his wig was askew, the audience was laughing and hissing and Mrs. Siddons covered her face with drapes, while she shook with suppressed laughter. Stephen Kemble was furious with Liston: he told him he had completely misinterpreted the character and threatened never to send him on stage again.[9]

Reluctantly, Kemble soon had to use Liston again, to replace the actor who usually played Diggory in *She Stoops to Conquer*. Liston worked carefully on the character and, when he appeared on stage wearing a white wig, the strands of which had been tied together by red tape, he was greeted by a shout of laughter from the *Gods*. He was surprised at the effect he created, for some of his fellow-actors could not stop laughing. The following morning Stephen Kemble called him into his office and asked him if he drank. When Liston replied that he did not, Kemble told him that, with time and study, he might make a comic actor, but he had not the face for it.[10]

When the company moved on to Newcastle, Liston appeared at the Newcastle Theatre for the first time. His debut took place on 3 August, when he played Gratiano in *The Merchant of Venice* and Sir Rowland, the wicked uncle, in Thomas Morton's *The Children in the Wood*. During his first season there he played a mixture of heavy father and low comedy parts, though he must have been amazed at the extraordinary state of the theatre. In all parts it was disagreeably dirty and most miserably lighted. The chandeliers at the back of the boxes regularly poured tallow over the hats and bonnets of those women unfortunate enough to be sitting directly beneath them. The scenery was old, shabby and dirty, and continually going wrong. The orchestra was inadequate, the prompter's voice could be frequently heard and, sometimes, the stage would be left vacant in the middle of an act for several minutes. The actors were an odd collection: Bew suffered from a speech impediment, Egerton moved jerkily, Stephen Kemble's range was limited by his excessive corpulence (he could play Falstaff without padding and was the fattest Hamlet on record) and the low comedian, Noble, was considered fit only for a barn or a farm yard. Only Kemble's wife won regular acclaim for her acting and the company was very dependent on visiting performers from London to boost its takings.[11]

Whatever the state of the theatre, Liston soon grew to like Newcastle's bustling, thriving community. He obtained lodgings at Mrs Cobbett's in Old Dispensary Yard, but later moved to Black-Bull entry, High-Bridge. In this house, in a narrow lane turning out of Pilgrim Street, Liston was very happy. The accommodation provided by the landlady, Mrs. Tarn, was very humble, but Liston always returned to his old lodgings whenever he visited Newcastle, even when he was rich and famous. On account of his gentlemanly demeanour and serious attitude to his profession, he soon became a favourite with both the Newcastle public and with the Kemble family. On the evening of 5 October, 1802, after Liston had amused the audience as Tony Lumpkin, Stephen Kemble's daughter made her debut in *Rosina*. Liston soon began to court the daughter, with whom he shared a delight in practical joking. His love for her was not to bring him much happiness, for she later rejected him for a Captain Arkwright, son of the cotton spinning magnate, financially a more satisfactory match. Liston did not forgive his rival lightly, often referring to him as a Captain in the *Malitia*.[12]

Liston played a wide range of roles whilst in Kemble's company. Not only did he play the "heavy" business (Darlemont in Holcroft's *Deaf and Dumb*, Pizarro in Sheridan's play), Shakespearian roles such as Kent, Banquo, Antonio in *The Merchant of Venice*, he also played an increasing number of low comedy roles, scoring particular success as John Lump in Colman's *The Review* and as Shenkin in Frederick Reynolds' *Folly as it Flies*. Yet, although Liston soon rose to prominence in the Newcastle company, he was dissatisfied with some of the conditions under which he had to perform. Not only was the salary poor, but the obligation to appear at different theatres in Kemble's circuit also caused difficulty. The circuit consisted, at this time, of Newcastle, Durham, North and South Shields, Scarborough and Sunderland. Particularly aggravating was a system then known as alternating performances. Whilst playing in Newcastle, the actors were expected to play at North Shields on alternate evenings. This system deprived the actors of time for such luxuries as rehearsals, since the greater part of each day was spent in walking along the turn-pike road between the two towns, often in inclement conditions. On receiving a complaint about this system from a group of actors, Kemble told them that they could leave as soon as they wished, for he could find actors as good as them in every bush. Later, as Kemble was driving along the turn-pike road in his carriage, he espied Liston standing in the middle of a hedge by the road-side. When he halted and asked him the reason for his extraordinary behaviour, Liston replied:

Only looking for some of the actors you told me of this morning.[13]

Perhaps it was dissatisfaction with such conditions that led Liston to negotiate with the eccentric Tate Wilkinson to join his company in York, in 1803. A few years earlier Wilkinson had lost his principal low comedian, John Emery, to one of the London theatres. Emery had long been a popular favourite in York, famed especially for his portrayal of cunning rustics and his mastery of the Yorkshire dialect; indeed, Emery's ascendancy in country roles led to the replacement of the traditional West Country accent assumed by stage rustics with the Yorkshire accent. Emery's greatest talent was an ability to play country roles so credibly and without exaggeration that he seemed to be the actual person he represented rather than a comic actor contriving comic effects. Emery had been replaced at York by Charles Mathews, whose lively and volatile style of acting won the hearts of the Yorkshire public. Mathews, like Emery, was eventually engaged by a London theatre, leaving Tate Wilkinson once more bereft of a low comedian.

Kemble was not happy about losing Liston and made difficulties over it. Wilkinson, who was continually losing his best performers as they were snapped up by London managements, felt aggrieved that Kemble should be so obdurate in similar circumstances. In the event Liston did not stay long at York. His first performance there, as John Lump, on 26 April, created little impact. The *York Herald* was later to state that it had been "led to expect something much above mediocrity", but that it had been disappointed. Charles Mathews and his wife met Liston and, although they found him likeable and gentlemanly, they were most impressed with his gravity, both on and off the stage. He didn't strike them as a very amusing performer and they were disappointed at the likelihood of his not becoming a great favourite. Shortly after Mathews and his wife had departed, Liston was involved in a dispute with Wilkinson. Edward Knight had taken over much of the low comedy business and Liston found himself required to play Irish characters and heavy fathers, available because of the sudden departure from the company of Denman. Liston found these characters totally unsuitable and threatened to resign. Wilkinson smoothed the matter over, but by June Liston was back in the Newcastle company, where he remained for the next two years.[14]

During these years the Newcastle Theatre was redecorated and the system of alternating performances was abolished. By 1804 Liston was leading the company in comedy and he must have been pleased with the favourable reviews he was receiving in the *Monthly Mirror*, which had been charting his progress over the years. In March, 1805, this journal considered that:

Mr. Liston is, if possible, a still greater favourite than ever. In country boys, in ridiculous old men, and in Mr. Fawcett's grotesque farcical characters, and comic songs, he is without a rival. He possesses a rich and sterling vein of comic humour, and whatever he performs, he is sure to render conspicuous and irresistably entertaining. Even in tragic characters, where no violent exertion is required, he is very respectable. He is yet young, and his natural good sense and remarkable diligence and attention to his profession, must in time lead him to a very distinguished situation in the theatrical world.

Liston's humour was not confined to the stage during these years. He also played a number of practical jokes back stage. During a performance of *Hamlet* he presented Mrs. Stephen Kemble with a basket of vegetables instead of the required flowers, as she stood dishevelled in the wings, ready to go on to perform Ophelia's mad scene. Fortunately the broad grin that spread across her features was assumed by the audience to be part of her interpretation. Mrs. Kemble was the victim of Liston's practical joking on another evening, when he painted Fanny's face like a clown's and planted her at a side-door next to the stage, just as her mother was about to perform a tragic scene: as soon as she caught a glimpse of her daughter's face, she burst out laughing.[15]

Many of the actors who visited the Newcastle circuit were struck by Liston's acting. Michael Kelly, the opera singer and composer, recommended him to the Drury Lane management, but nothing came of it. Charles Kemble, with whom Liston frequently played when he visited Newcastle, suggested to George Colman the younger that he invite Liston to join the Haymarket company for the summer season of 1805. Colman followed his advice and, on 24 May, 1805, Liston found himself making his final appearance before the Newcastle public.

During his years with Stephen Kemble he had advanced from obscurity to pre-eminence as a low comedian. The range of experience and grounding in technique that he obtained here stood him in good stead for the rest of his career: without this initial apprenticeship he would probably have failed to make so remarkable and original a contribution to the theatre of his time. Years later, when he paid his professional farewell visit to Newcastle, he told the citizens that it was their "fostering protection that first pointed the road to fame and fortune" and that he looked back "with gratitude to the kindness he had always received from them, his earliest patrons".[16]

Chapter II

London Debut – 1805–1808

One summer evening in 1805 the streets of Charing Cross were thronged with people walking in a westerly direction. They were, as usual, on their way to Colman's little theatre in the Haymarket, the only theatre in London licensed for summer entertainment. That particular evening, Monday 10 June, they were to see a rather old-fashioned comedy by William Macready,* *The Village Lawyer*. A new comedian was to make his debut in the character of Sheepface – John Liston from the Newcastle Theatre. Not that there was anything special about this. New comedians were often allowed to make a debut at the Haymarket Theatre, only to fade into oblivion immediately afterwards.

John Liston was undoubtedly nervous as he left his lodgings at the Orange Coffee House, Cockspur Street. Dressed in his favourite pea-green coat he walked the short distance to the Haymarket Theatre, followed by a little pug dog which trotted along behind him. Some of the cast were already in the green-room when he arrived – it was literally a green-room, into which light was admitted by a thing like a cucumber-frame at one end of it. Charles Mathews was there: he was to play Scout, a cunning lawyer, and had been placed in a rather embarrassing position by the arrival of Liston. Colman, the manager, had asked Mathews what he knew of Liston, before engaging him for the summer season. Mathews had not found Liston particularly comical when he had acted with him at York and felt unable to recommend him to Colman with much enthusiasm.

Another habituee of the green-room was Colman's wife, Mrs. Gibbs. She recalled the first time Liston had visited the theatre. He had been sitting in the green-room, deep in thought, when she had walked in. His chin was resting on his stick and between his legs, also apparently deep in thought, was his pug dog. The effect was so ludicrous that she had to rush out of the green-room roaring with laughter. She explained to some of her

* father of the famous tragedian

11

fellow-actors that she was laughing so much because "there was a man and a dog in the room whose physiognomies were so exactly alike, it was hard to tell which was which".[1]

Nervously, dressed as the gawky country booby who outwits the scheming lawyer, Liston awaited his appearance before the Haymarket public. The audience was merry, crammed into the well-constructed pit of the theatre, and, as soon as the stage lights rose, it brightened even more. At the third sounding, when the orchestra struck up, the delight was immense and, once the play had begun, hands rose instinctively to welcome old favourites. In so small an auditorium reminisced George Daniel, to whom we owe this description of the Haymarket audience, the rapport between actors and audience was very close and not a look, gesture or syllable was lost.

Mathews need not have worried. Liston's acting took him so completely by surprise, he was convulsed with laughter and was scarcely able to utter a word intelligibly, whilst they were on stage together. Liston himself was not quite so happy. The following morning he waited on James Winston, the stage manager, his wardrobe tied in a spotted handkerchief and his ugly little dog beside him. He requested that his articles of agreement might be cancelled, as he felt he would never reach the standards demanded by a London audience. He wished to return to the North, where he now felt more at home. Winston, never the most accommodating of men, observed that he had no power to cancel the engagement without the consent of Colman and that Colman was not available. So Liston stayed and he was soon able to console himself by reading the account of his performance in the *Monthly Mirror* (July, 1805), which praised the quiet style of acting and lack of exaggeration with which he portrayed Sheepface's archness and simplicity.

Liston's engagement at the Haymarket Theatre continued throughout the summer. He played mainly rustic characters in a series of competent, if undistinguished, performances. However, if he was to remain in London, he would have to look to an engagement at either Covent Garden or Drury Lane during the winter months, when these were the only two theatres permitted to open. During the summer the press had maintained that he was a strong candidate for employment at one of the winter theatres and it was Covent Garden, finally, that took him on, at a salary of £6 per week. He made his debut on Tuesday 15 October, as Jacob *Pls. 2(b), 2(d)* Gawkey in *The Chapter of Accidents*. Gawkey was another country bumpkin, whom Liston invested with just the right degree of vacancy and stupidity. He looked as if every turn of his limbs had been copied from the farm yard and seemed quite unconscious of the mirth he was creating around him. Even Charles Kemble, who as a love-sick swain should have been in an agony of despair, could not stop laughing. Although the house was only half-full, successive peals of applause followed Liston's exit.[2]

Liston was pleased with the reception accorded him at Covent Garden, but he was upset by one reaction. A critic in one of the papers cavilled at his performance, and wished to know with affected ignorance where *"the managers had picked him up"* to which he replied, by letter, *"Sir, I was picked up in the Haymarket"*. From that time on he paid very little attention to criticism and avoided much annoyance through doing so.[3]

Although the engagement at Covent Garden was prestigious, Liston found he had very little to do during his first few seasons. There were already a number of established low comedians in the company, monopolising most of the low comedy roles. Munden was probably the most outstanding, though John Emery, specialising in Yorkshire rustics, was also quite prominent. Then there was John Fawcett, who had built his reputation on playing volatile and eccentric characters. Most comic roles in tragedy and melodrama were bespoken: the only hope for a new low comedian was to have roles especially written for him; and, consequently, Liston was at first under-used at Covent Garden. Some of the company began to feel that his engagement had been unwise, for his performances subsequent to Jacob Gawkey had not been very successful. The general consensus was that he had a comical face, but that his technique was inadequate. At times his performances seemed cold and spiritless, giving no hint at all of the rich comic genius that lay buried within.

Liston had joined the Covent Garden company at an inauspicious time. Not only was the company already well supplied with low comedians, its repertoire was limited by the insatiable craze for the boy actor, Master Betty. Even John Philip Kemble had decided to take second place whilst the Betty mania raged, still almost at fever-pitch, during the 1805–6 season. Even so, Liston found himself playing a number of new roles, including the cowardly Memmo in "Monk" Lewis's new drama, *Rugantino*, and also Gaby Grim, especially created for him by Colman in a new comedy, *We Fly by Night*. He even took over Munden's old role of Governor Tempest in Cumberland's *The Wheel of Fortune*, famous for Kemble's performance as the dreary recluse, Penruddock. Such roles allowed him to make little impact on the public, but at least the artist De Wilde realised his potential, depicting Liston as Jacob Gawkey, Gaby Grim and as two stock-characters in plays by Isaac Jackman, Diggory in *All the World's a Stage* and Solomon in *The Quaker*.[4]   *Pl. 5(a)*

Only when he returned to the Haymarket for another summer season did Liston come into his own once more. Charles Mathews was there again and he and Liston fast became close friends. Although their styles of acting were very different, they blended well together, a feature that was noted by the youthful playwright, Theodore Hook. Writer, punster and practical joker, Hook wrote a number of comedies for the Haymarket Theatre purely to exploit the Mathews-Liston partnership. His play *Catch Him Who Can* was one of the hits of the 1806 season. Mathews was a servant, who had to resort to a series of disguises in order to get a letter to an imprisoned Count. The Count is guarded by a foolish soldier, Jeffrio de Pedrillos, played by Liston. Self-complacent, conceited, sure that all women must find him attractive, Liston conveyed, through look and gesture, a total sense of vanity and ignorance. In future seasons *The Fortress, Music Mad* and *Killing No Murder* were further vehicles by which Hook helped to contribute to the reputation of both performers. Mathews' characters were always alert and lively, masters of disguise, ever taking advantage of some dupe or another; Liston's characters were slow, often stupid, eternal victims. Hook very much saw the characters he created as sketches for the two actors, which they would then fill in.[5] Yet, however lightly he wrote in their parts, he played an important part in enhancing the reputation of both actors and in shaping the direction of their future careers.

This was the great age of hoaxers and Hook was one of the greatest exponents of them all. One evening he procured several orders to admit to the Haymarket a young gentleman, the son of a knight, who was anxious to escort to the theatre a young female cousin, with whom he was carrying on a flirtation. The young gentleman did not dare mention the visit to his father, a stern presbyterian, with strong views about the theatre. Hook obtained seats for them in the front row of the dress circle, where their faces would be inconspicuous to most of the audience. He also informed Liston, who was performing that night, about what he had done. During a burst of laughter when he was on stage, Liston advanced to the footlights and looking around the dress circle with a grave and offended air, exclaimed:

"I don't understand this conduct, ladies and gentlemen! I am not accustomed to be laughed at! I can't imagine what you see ridiculous in *me*! Why, I declare, there's Harry B-, too, and his cousin, Martha J".

As he spoke, he pointed at the centre of the dress circle.

"What business have they to come here and laugh at me, I should like to know! I'll go and tell his father, and see what he thinks of it!"

The couple were so alarmed by the number of people that turned to look at them, that they left their seats and rushed out of the theatre.[6]

On another occasion Liston was the object of one of Hook's practical jokes. The other hit of the 1806 season was Thomas Dibdin's *Five Miles Off* or *The Finger Post*, in which Liston played Flourish, a Quaker. He was praised for the dry humour with which he played this role and for avoiding the conventional clichés associated with Quaker roles. Particularly amusing was a song (Quakers were forbidden to sing), "When I fell into the pit of love". During a performance of this play Hook made his way under the stage, with a bladder attached to a penny whistle. He then introduced the orifice of the tube of this instrument, which in sound resembled a bagpipe, through a gap in the platform, close to where Liston's feet were placed, just before he was about to sing his song, "When I fell into the pit of love". As he sang he was accompanied by a discordant squeak, much to his mystification, for he could not locate its source. The audience was highly amused, insisting on an encore, which was again accompanied by this mysterious sound.[7]

Apart from the association with Hook and Mathews, Liston's career did not advance very much in these early years. His second season at Covent Garden provided him with fewer opportunities than his first and, once Grimaldi had scored a great success in his first Covent Garden pantomime, *Harlequin and Mother Goose*, there was little need for the sort of play in which Liston appeared. Still, there was one consolation. During his first season at the Haymarket a short, plump actress, with the sweetest of dispositions and a very pleasant singing voice, often played opposite him. Her name was Sarah Tyrer and she had been born on 6 May, 1781, the daughter of a watchmaker who was also a rigid presbyterian. Her father, who was strongly prejudiced against the stage, died when she was about fourteen. The family was now impoverished, but a lady who had been impressed by Sarah's singing talents placed her as a pupil with the celebrated Mrs. Crouch.[8] After receiving singing lessons both from Mrs. Crouch and from Michael Kelly, she made her first recorded appearance at Drury Lane on 21 May, 1801, when she played Fidelia in *The Pirates* for Mrs. Crouch's benefit.[9] A month later she made her debut at the Haymarket Theatre. She specialised in simple, unaffected country girls and servants, especially if they were required to sing, and she was also very successful in burlesque.

Sarah Tyrer was first engaged at Covent Garden in 1805, the same year that Liston joined the company. She was extremely short, well under five feet, and very jolly, making a strong contrast with the new comedian, who was tall, well-built, always exquisitely dressed and generally pensive. They got to know each other well and Liston eventually proposed marriage. The wedding took place at the parish church of St. Martin's in the Fields on 22 March, 1807, just after Covent Garden had closed down for the Easter recess. After a wedding breakfast provided by their friend Charles Taylor the Listons moved to their first home together at 25 Great Russell Street. Their marriage was to prove very happy: Sarah was not only good-hearted, but also a shrewd business-woman, even saving her husband from heavy losses on one occasion.[10] One memoir described how her "sweetness of disposition, amiable temper, and unaffected goodness of heart, made her the delight of all who know her, and the subject of heartfelt praise to the many to whom her kindness has been extended".[11] In public she could also be modest and retiring. Once, at the baptism of Sheridan's grandson, she feigned illness because she felt too shy to comply with the Prince of Wales' desire that she should sing.[12]

Shortly after their marriage Liston and his wife played opposite each other at the Haymarket in Hook's new play *The Fortress*, first performed on 16 July. Liston played a one-eyed sergeant called Philip and at one point he had to oppose the entry of his wife into the fortress with the words:

"You can't pass this way, Miss".

Her reply was:

"Miss, indeed! I'll have you know I'm no miss!"

The audience applauded these lines, applying them to Liston's recent marriage. Sarah was so disconcerted that she burst into tears and retired upstage. Liston went up to her, took her apron and wiped her eyes, but his ludicrous expression of concern drew as much laughter as applause.[13]

A few days later Liston was invited to dine at a certain Dr. Batty's. Winston, the Haymarket stage manager, was also of the company and was alarmed to see Liston drinking the wine very freely, since he was due to play Lord Grizzle in *Tom Thumb* later that evening. Charles Mathews had given up the part several years before because he could do nothing with it. Liston had taken over the role, but he had never been very successful either, which was perhaps the reason for his vast intake of alchohol on that particular evening. In fact Liston refused to set off for the Haymarket at all, so that eventually Winston almost had to drag him there. They arrived with only a few minutes to spare and Liston hurriedly donned the old-fashioned costume and long wig of the solemnly severe and pompous Lord Grizzle. Once on stage, inspired by the wine, he felt inclined to exaggerate more than usual and, when he had completed the song "In Hurry Post Haste for a License", he broke into a grotesque comic *Pl. 3* dance.[14] The audience was ecstatic and *Tom Thumb* became one of the hits of the season. At last, it seemed, Liston had begun to find a comic style that could really pull in the audiences.

Years later Hazlitt wrote about the energy and exuberance with which Liston performed in this burlesque, which was, incidentally, an adaptation by Kane O'Hara from Fielding's original play:

> His Lord Grizzle is prodigious. What a name, and what a person! It has been said of this ingenious actor that he is "very great in Liston"; but he is even greater in Lord Grizzle. What a wig is that he wears! How flighty, flaunting and fantastical! ... His wits seem flying away with the disorder of his flowing locks, and to sit as loosely on our hero's head as the cawl of his peruke. What a significant vacancy in his open eye and mouth! What a listlessness in his limbs! What an abstraction of all thought or purpose! With what a headlong impulse of enthusiasm he throws himself across the stage when he is going to be married, crying "Hey for Doctor's Commons"; as if the genius of folly had taken full-length possession of his person! And then his dancing is equal to the discovery of a sixth sense, which is certainly different from *common* sense. If this extra-ordinary personage cuts a figure in his life, he is no less wonderful in his death and burial. From the sublime to the ridiculous there is but one step; and the character would almost seem to prove, that there is but one step from the ridiculous to the sublime.[15]

Burlesque became very popular and in August, 1807, Sheridan's *The Critic* was revived, with all its theatrical allusions altered and made applicable to the Haymarket. Mathews was very successful as Puff and Liston as Don Whiskerandos caused much amusement when, after vigorously encoring his death scene by rolling all over the earth like a scorched fly, he expostulated that he could not stay dying all night. Sarah Liston contributed to the general mayhem as Queen Tilburina. Her burlesque performances were very popular: she played Queen Dollalolla in *Tom Thumb* as a bossy, scolding woman, "singing her songs with much vulgar dignity".[16] As Tilburina she was equally impressive.

Pl. 4(a)

After Liston and Mathews had appeard in *Music Mad*, especially written by Hook for Mathews' Haymarket benefit on 27 August, Liston once again returned to Covent Garden. So popular was Liston's Lord Grizzle that *Tom Thumb* was revived and frequently performed during the new season. One evening the audience demanded a third encore of Liston's grotesque dance. Some of them were displeased when Liston came forward to tell them that he was too fatigued to do any more dancing. During the fight scene someone called out from the audience, "Don't do too much, you'll fatigue him". The next day a bulletin appeared in the green-room announcing – "Lord Grizzle's physicians are happy to announce his Lordship is greatly recovered from his fatigue".[17] Liston's comic dancing became a feature of many of his early parts. In volatile mood he would parody the dancing of the Corps de Ballet at the King's Theatre: this was very funny, especially as he was practically double-jointed and helped by "a natural looseness of the hips".[18]

Pl. 5(b)   Liston's comic dancing was at the centre of his first major success at Covent Garden: Caper in J. T. Allingham's *Who Wins*, first performed on 25 February, 1808. As one critic put it, "Liston's legs ran away with most of the applause".[19] Without doing the precise steps, he managed to give a perfect notion of the ingeniously wriggling contortions of the Corps de Ballet. His looseness of limb converted the graceful and beautiful motions of the original dancers into a grotesque comic parody. It was not just dancing that made this new character a hit: there was something original about it as well. Caper was a rich, provincial merchant, an affected coxcomb, enriched financially but not intellectually as a result of the industrial revolution. This type of character, vain, rich, cowardly, stupid, was something very special to Liston. The country bumpkins, whom he had played when he first arrived in London, were soon replaced by characters like Caper. Hazlitt, comparing Liston's Lord Grizzle with his Caper, wrote "Caper can alone dispute the palm with its incoherence and its volatility; for that, too, is "high fantastical", almost as full of emptiness, in as grand a gusto of insipidity, as profoundly absurd, as elaborately nonsensical"!![20] According to Oxberry's *Memoir* "the impression Liston made as Caper was not easily forgotten: it helped to lay the foundations of a favour scarcely ever afforded any other performer by the public".[21]

Caper ensured Liston of greater prominence within the Covent Garden company, but even before this he had achieved considerable critical recognition. He was praised for his originality, for his ability to immerse himself within the character he was playing and heralded as a great popular favourite. The critic Leigh Hunt indicated his quality in the essay devoted to Liston in his *Critical Essays on the Performers of the London Stage*, which was published in 1807. He praised Liston in both affected and rustic roles:

> His accuracy of conception enables him to represent with equal felicity the most true characters and the most affected habits, and he passes from the simplest rustic to the most conceited pretender with undiminished easiness of attainment. The actor never carries him beyond the characteristic strength of his part; he adds nothing of stage affectation and diminishes nothing of nature; yet his manner is so irresolutely

Plate 1 John Liston: portrait by J. Jackson

Plate 2 Liston: (a) top left, as Paul Pry; (b) top right, as Jacob Gawkey in *The Chapter of Accidents*; (c) bottom left, as Pompey in *Measure for Measure*; (d) bottom right, as Jacob Gawkey

Plate 3 Liston as Lord Grizzle in *Tom Thumb*

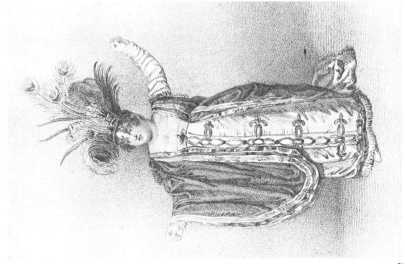

a

b

Plate 4 Mrs. Liston: (a) left, as Queen Dollalolla in *Tom Thumb*; (b) right, as Madge in *Love in a Village*

Plate 5 Liston: (a) left, as Diggory in *All the World's a Stage*; (b) right, as Caper in *Who Wins*

Plate 6 Liston as Baron Altradoff in *The Exile*

Plate 7   Liston as Apollo Belvi in *Killing no Murder*

The Miller and his Men.

Karl. They've caught a Tartar, sir, that's all.

Act II. Scene I.

Plate 8 Scene from *The Miller and his Men*

humorous, that he can put the audience into good humour with less effort than any other comedian.[22]

Liston's easy, effortless style of acting was particularly noticeable in his affected roles:

> In more youthful characters of little vigour, whose chief quality is a mixture of ignorance and self-complacency, Mr Liston indulges in his proper feebleness. There may be observed a general repose of limb and of intellect in his style of acting exquisitely conducive to the character of contented folly; he can seem at ease with all around him, but most voluptuously so with himself: his smile of self-conceit is most peculiarly significant and enjoying. ...[23]

Leigh Hunt did not feel Liston was as adequate when it came to playing old men and, after careful comparison, decided that Emery had the edge on Liston in country roles. Overall, though, he would probably have concurred with the view expressed a year later that Liston had "already become one of the greatest favourites on the stage".[24]

There was no doubt about Liston's popularity by the summer of 1808. He was much in demand at Covent Garden benefits, as both an actor and a singer of comic songs. One song that proved a particular favourite was "A Frog He Would a Wooing Go". Another song that became popular throughout the British Isles during the summer of 1808 was sung by Liston as Henry Augustus Mug, a cockney wood and ivory turner in Colman's new play *The Africans*, which had become the major attraction at the Haymarket Theatre. "Won't you Come, Mr. Mug?" was frequently encored and Liston's performance was considered the main strength of the production. After only three years the snub-nosed, red-cheeked comedian with his solemn demeanour and freedom from excess had achieved prominence among the comedy actors of the day.

Chapter III

The Rise to Fame – 1808–1815

One night in the autumn of 1808 many Londoners were awoken by an orange, incandescent glow in the sky and, in the vicinity of Covent Garden, by a great deal of hustle and bustle. The Covent Garden Theatre was ablaze and, in no time at all, had burnt to the ground. Twenty three people had been killed, mostly by the collapse of the theatre's burning roof. Whatever the cause of the fire, the destruction was almost total. The last play to be performed there had been Charles Kemble's *Plot and Counterplot*, in which Liston played Pedrillo.

The Covent Garden company continued to perform, first at the King's Theatre, then at Colman's little theatre in the Haymarket. Among the new plays written to help the homeless company was Frederick Reynolds' *The Exile*, a spectacular drama in which Liston played an eccentric *Pl. 6* traveller, Baron Altradoff, and created much mirth in a comic duet with Munden, who was cast as the Governor of Siberia. In the meantime Covent Garden Theatre was rebuilt at a cost of approximately £150,000 and was ready to re-open within a year. John Philip Kemble, co-proprietor of the theatre with Thomas Harris, had rather exceeded the resources available in order to make this possible in so short a time; so, to recoup the losses, the management raised the prices and engaged the celebrated opera singer, Madame Catalani. Moreover, the best part of the new theatre had been given over to the provision of private boxes for the aristocracy. This caused general disapproval and, when Kemble came forward to speak the prologue on the opening night of the 1809–10 season, he could hardly make himself heard. *Macbeth*, chosen as the opening play, was scarcely audible through the din. Liston, when he appeared in that night's afterpiece, *The Quaker*, was greeted by a few cheers, but the disturbances continued and he was nearly hit by a candle. After the curtain went down, the audience continued to demonstrate for another two hours.

The Old Price Riots, as they were to be called, continued for most of that year. The opposition to the raised prices was well-organised and sustained. Among the more prominent figures to be attacked were Madame Catalani and Kemble, against whom most of the dissension was directed. The fact that the protesters were against the private boxes also turned the dispute into a social issue and Brandon, the boxkeeper, was frequently abused. The newspapers and periodicals devoted columns to blow by blow accounts of the proceedings, complete with details of each slogan imprinted on banners waved the night before, and multiplied considerably the space usually given to theatrical affairs. The arguments often led to fights, not surprisingly, since gangs of hired ruffians were usually present in the theatre.

On Saturday 21 October Liston's attention was drawn to a letter in *The Statesman*. He was most indignant to find himself cited in the controversy by an anonymous correspondent, who had written:

> I was this evening sitting in a public coffee room with a friend; it was publicly stated by a Gentleman then present, that Mr. Liston had said, in a mixed company, that the Managers of Covent Garden Theatre would have carried the point of the new prices, but for the opposition of the *blackguard* citizens.

Liston was asked to refute this charge, which showed "an atrocious mixture of affected consequence and base ingratitude". Angrily, Liston replied from the address to which he had recently moved in the Strand, stating that the so-called *gentleman* had *knowingly* uttered "a gross and malicious falsehood".[1] Yet, in spite of Liston's refutation, the seeds of discord were sown. On November 11 a gentleman in the Covent Garden pit harangued the audience and referred to the application of the word *Blackguard* by Liston to the citizens of London. He considered it to be shameful that the inhabitants of London, while supporting their country's triumphant navy, should be so abused. Before he had time to finish, a disturbance arose in another part of the house.

Two days later Liston and the veteran singer, Incledon, appeared together in *The Quaker*. Liston was greeted with a tremendous roar of indignation when he appeared and he and Incledon were pelted with apples. So sustained was the outcry that Liston advanced to the front of the stage, at the end of the first act, and requested a hearing. Eventually a semblance of silence was obtained and the demonstrators in the pit seated themselves, though Liston was frequently interrupted as he spoke. He referred to the letter in *The Statesman* and assured the audience that the accusations had been unfounded. How, he said, could he insult a public for whose patronage and favours he was so grateful. By the time he had finished speaking the audience was on his side and cheered loudly. When *The Quaker* was resumed, the uproar was hushed for a short time, as tribute to the open and honourable way in which Liston had addressed the audience. His diplomatic handling of the incident had turned it into a personal triumph.

Other problems had been thrown up earlier that year. During the summer Liston had been engaged at the Haymarket, as usual, with Charles Mathews. Theodore Hook had written a new musical farce especially for them, but, after it had been advertised numerous times, it was mysteriously withdrawn. The problem, it transpired, lay in the character of Apollo Belvi, a Methodist dancing master from Swansea, to be played by Liston. Belvi, a hypocritical, foolish and self-seeking individual, provided the play with its title, *Killing No Murder*, for he pretends to be dead in order to avoid what he fears will be an unsuitable marriage. The Examiner of plays, Larpent, himself a Methodist, refused to license the play on the grounds that it was a shameful and indecent attack on a very harmless group of people. Hook had to agree to changes in the text, before Larpent would issue a license. He was not unduly perturbed by this, since Larpent's action had created a lot of advance publicity for the play.

When the play was at last performed, it proved a great success. Mathews, as Buskin, an unemployed actor, dominated the first half of the play; not only was there plenty of opportunity to display his facility in disguising himself, but he also introduced for the first time the popular "Mail Coach Song". Liston, who came into his own in the second half, *Pl. 7* was a great hit as the affected Belvi, a mixture of cunning, naivety and simplicity. Outwitted by Buskin into relinquishing his intended bride, he provided much amusement as the centre of the farcical intrigue. The audience roared, in particular, as he sang and danced to the following lines:

> Twisting, twirling, body bending
> Nimbly o'er the boards we go,
> No pipes equal hornpipes truly,
> On the light fantastic toe.
> Shuffling, cutting, cap'ring, strutting
> Entrechat de six you know,
> Then your arms like teapot putting
> Thus you twirl your straightened toe.

Apollo Belvi remained in Liston's repertoire for many years, reputedly one of his favourite parts.

Further difficulties arose at the Haymarket during ensuing summer seasons. David Morris, Colman's brother-in-law and co-proprietor, considered that George Colman the younger was extravagant, especially over the terms he was prepared to offer some of his summer performers, and wanted him divested of his responsibilities. He also resented the fact that Colman preferred to write new plays for the winter theatres, since his earnings did not then deplete his takings as a manager. In January, 1810, he placed an advertisement in the newspapers, reminding all performers, except the Listons, that their engagements had terminated during the previous September.[2] Colman ignored this open declaration of hostility and went ahead in engaging artists of his own choice for the summer season. Morris retaliated in 1811, when Colman did the same thing again, by withholding the wages of any actors to whose engagement he had not agreed. Munden, Robert Elliston and Richard Jones, who were the victims of Morris's decision, then refused to act. The difficulties were eventually resolved, but the battle between Colman and Morris for control of the theatre continued for several years more.

Little of note was produced at the Haymarket during the 1810 and 1811 seasons. A number of new burlesques were staged, the aftermath of the successful revivals of *Tom Thumb* and *The Critic*, and these constituted the main attractions. In 1810 Liston played the name part in *Bombastes Furioso*, a rather feeble burlesque by a bank clerk, William Barnes Rhodes.   *Pl. 11*
Rhodes had borrowed the mock heroic form of burlesque, but unlike his predecessors had found nothing specific to parody. Still, it proved popular enough and Liston, as the histrionic General, achieved an amusing parody of Madame Catalani in the song "Hope Told a Flattering Tale". The following year Liston appeared with Munden in *The Quadrupeds of Quedlinbergh,* a satire on Sheridan's *Pizarro* and on the fashion for equestrian drama. Colman knocked this piece together from *The Rovers* by George Canning and John Hookham Frere, a burlesque first published in *The Anti-Jacobin* in 1799. Liston played Rogero, in love with Matilda Pottingen and a prisoner in a subterranean vault for eleven long years. Rogero was a ludicrous role, but not as extreme as one of the parts Liston undertook for a Covent Garden benefit in 1813. On this occasion he played a burlesque Ophelia in John Poole's *Hamlet Travestie.*

By 1812 Liston had had enough of the Haymarket. The differences between Morris and Colman were still unresolved and the prospect of reliable summer employment there seemed slight. He had also been irritated at the beginning of the previous season when Colman had put pressure on him to perform, even though he was feeling unwell.[3] So, rather than return again to the Haymarket, he decided upon a tour of the provinces instead. Not that travelling across country was much to be

relished, even in summer. Admittedly, roads were at last being con-
structed on sound principles and the muddy old quagmires that had once
functioned as highways were disappearing. Coaches could travel more
efficiently, with less discomfort to their passengers, but a journey across
England could still be a time-consuming and perilous enterprise. Liston
hardly enjoyed the inconveniences of this sort of travel, but for leading
actors the greatest profits were to be reaped in the provinces, whatever the
hardships of the travel involved. He returned to the Newcastle circuit,
where he was rapturously received, and then progressed to Liverpool for
another fortnight. He and his wife, who had made special appearances at
his Newcastle and Liverpool benefits, then returned to London a week
before the new season at Covent Garden was due to commence.

The previous two seasons at Covent Garden had not provided Liston
with many memorable new roles. He had played Malvolio for the first
time and the silly part of Macloon in *The Knight of Snowdoun*, an adaptation
by Thomas Morton of Scott's *The Lady of the Lake*. More successful had
been Neddy Bray, a foolish provincial who comes to London in search of a
wife, in Colman's *XYZ*. Described as "another of those oddities written
expressedly for Liston and conspicuous only in his hands",[4] it provided
many opportunities for awkwardness, bashfulness and cross-purpose.
After two performances however it was withdrawn. Morris brought an
injunction to prevent its performance at Covent Garden and the play
became the subject of a Chancery suit. Several years later, in a much
abbreviated version, it proved very successful when it was revived at the
Haymarket.

The new season at Covent Garden augured well. Liston was delighted
that his old friend Charles Mathews was to be a member of the company.
Mathews had been engaged to replace Munden, who had quarrelled with
the management over his salary and defected to Drury Lane. For his
debut Mathews chose *Killing No Murder*, which immediately partnered
him with Liston again. Before long the two of them appeared in a revival
Pls. 9, 10   of John Burgoyne's comedy, *The Lord of the Manor*. Liston played Moll
Flaggon, a gin-drinking, pipe-smoking camp follower, with such effect
that the role remained in his repertoire for the next twenty years. Within
three weeks of this revival, on 20 November 1812, Liston and Mathews
appeared together again, in a new play by James Kenney, *Love, Law and
Physic*.

Kenney was a very talented playwright, technically adept at crafting
both comedy and melodrama, but he suffered from ill-health and a very
nervous disposition. He found it difficult to make up his mind over the
smallest things, whether it was stepping over a puddle or climbing into a
carriage. He had a large family to support and was always short of money,

but he was a perfect gentleman and an amusing companion.[5] His new farce provided Mathews with an excellent part – the lawyer Flexible – and, in Lubin Log, he provided Liston with one of the most important roles of his career. So complete was Liston's identification with the role that Hazlitt found it hard to say "whether the soul of Liston has passed into Mr. Lubin Log, or that of Mr. Lubin Log into Mr. Liston", since there was "a most wonderful congeniality and mutual good understanding" between them.[6] *Pls. 12, 13*

Lubin Log was very like Caper and Apollo Belvi – conceited, stupid, vulgar, cowardly – but he was something else as well – a cockney. This was not the first cockney character Liston had played, for Mug in Colman's *The Africans* had also been a cockney. Lubin Log, however, was cockneyism personified and the lower middle-class cockney, complacently aware of London's superiority to all other places, was to be one of Liston's major contributions to the nineteenth century stage. He created a series of characters very like the typical cockney that Hazlitt describes in one of his essays:

> He sees everything near, superficial, little, in hasty succession. The world turns round, and his head with it, like a roundabout at a fair ... he sees and hears a vast number of things and knows nothing. He is pert, raw, ignorant, conceited, ridiculous, shallow, contemptible. His senses keep him alive; and he knows, inquires and cares for nothing further ... He despises the country, because he is ignorant of it, and the town, because he is familiar with it. He is ... a great man in proxy ... surcharged with a sort of second-hand, vapid, tingling, troublesome self-importance. His personal vanity is thus continually flattered and perked up with ridiculous self-complacency, while his imagination is jaded and impaired by daily abuse. Everything is vulgarised in his mind ... Let him be as low as he will, he fancies he is as good as anybody else. ...[7]

Liston did for this sort of cockney what John Emery had already done for the cunning Yorkshireman. Interestingly enough, Emery played a Yorkshireman in *Love, Law and Physic*, outwitting the conceitedly superior Log with his native guile.

Although Lubin Log was an original creation, Liston found part of his inspiration at a dinner party he attended. One of the guests was a vulgar cockney who always made an exhibition of himself on these occasions. Liston watched him carefully and, when he made his debut as Lubin Log, reproduced some of the man's characteristics.[8] So convincing was Liston's portrayal of cockney vulgarity that some of his audience found no merit in his performance: it was just as if one of their acquaintances had walked onto the stage and talked and behaved in his usual manner. Boastful, mean, ludicrously costumed, Lubin Log was to remain one of Liston's most popular parts and point the way for many more cockney characters.

Lubin Log, who has just inherited a large fortune, travels to York by coach in order to marry a young lady named Laura. The match has been arranged by her father, who is horrified by Log's vulgarity when he meets him for the first time. Laura's preferred suitor, a young man called Danvers, happens to travel north on the same coach as Log, but seated outside. His friend Flexible, the lawyer, travels within and discovers Log's purpose in coming to York. He schemes with Danvers to forestall the marriage through a series of deceptions designed to convince Log that he has been disinherited. With the aid of an actress, another passenger on the coach, Flexible finally tricks Log into renouncing his intention of marrying Laura.

Liston put a tremendous amount of detail into his performance of Log. On his first appearance he wore a short black coat with covered buttons, a striped waistcoat and a belcher handkerchief tied around his head, on top of which was a small, queer-looking hat. His appearance was ridiculous, a feature further accentuated by wearing black jack-boots, above which striped stockings were showing. His fingers, said the *Drama*, were well acquainted with every inch of his dress: he knew exactly where to dive for sixpence as well as where to feel for his nose. His coat seemed an old friend and almost a part of himself.[9] In the second act, when his travelling attire was changed for something more elegant, he looked even more outrè, in an awkwardly-fitting powdered wig and a rather long waistcoat, which seemed "emulous of his knees".[10]

In such roles Liston seemed able to absorb himself in the most petty circumstances. All his energies were deployed, without bustle or passion, in a concentrated attempt to deal with some trivial annoyance. In so doing he satirised the lofty pretensions of humanity and presented "a stronger and truer picture of the littleness of man".[11] As Lubin Log he made his first appearance shortly after alighting from the coach, followed onto the stage by the coachman, who is waiting for his tip. Log detains the coachman, as he finds him a sixpence, in order to impress upon him that a tip is by no means a compulsory measure, but a pure and spontaneous emanation of generosity, or, in his own phrase, "Quite hoptional!" In his countenance Liston displayed "the vital importance he attaches to what he is about"[12] and the "knowing style" and "satisfactory composure"[13] with which he accomplished his object caused great amusement. Liston's performance was filled with moments as memorable and well-observed as this one, so much so that it looked as if "the manners of Log were engrafted in him".[14] "A more perfect personation", said Hazlitt, "we never witnessed. The happy compound of meaness, ignorance, vulgarity and conceit, was given with the broadest effect, and with the nicest discrimination of feeling".[15] According to the *Examiner*(14/3/1813) Lubin Log was rendered by Liston "with a force and truth and shews that he possesses the most intelligent relish for humour, and a power of expressing it, quite unequalled on the stage".

After the Covent Garden season had closed Liston and his wife undertook an engagement at the Lyceum – the English Opera – in the Strand. This differed from the Haymarket, which remained closed during the summer of 1813 whilst Colman and Morris fought a protracted suit in Chancery, in that it concentrated on comic opera rather than on comedy and farce. Fanny Kelly, the actress with whom Charles Lamb was much enamoured, was also in the company. She and Liston scored a great success, when they re-engaged for the 1814 season, in *Harlequin Hoax*, an afterpiece especially written by Thomas Dibdin. In this they both played themselves: a new author has had the temerity to cast them as Harlequin and Columbine and they plan their revenge upon him. A slight, but amusing piece, *Harlequin Hoax* gently satirised the excesses of the annual Harlequinades and proved the major attraction of the season.

Samuel Arnold, the manager of the English Opera House, had first obtained a licence to open during the summer months in 1812. He had secured the services of Liston and his wife for four, not necessarily consecutive, summers. The winter theatres, however, were jealous of the initial success of the venture: they saw it as a threat and wished to suppress it. Drury Lane threatened any performers who engaged at the Lyceum that they would forfeit their winter engagements. At the opening of the 1816 season the Listons were prohibited by the Proprietors of Covent Garden from fulfilling their obligations to appear at the Lyceum. They were threatened with heavy penalties or even dismissal from the theatre, despite the fact that Covent Garden had made no objections at all to their previous engagements.[16]

Back at Covent Garden Liston had continued to play not only in comedy and farce, but also in classical revivals and in melodramas. In the autumn of 1813 he played in one of the most outstanding melodramas of the age, *The Miller and His Men*. It was a strange period in British history: the wars with France had lasted for around twenty years, initiated before Liston had ever set foot on a stage professionally. Oddly enough the wars had contributed to the prosperity then enjoyed by the British theatre, which in turn supported the war effort through the patriotic songs and dramas frequently performed. Throughout the autumn and winter of 1813 there was great jubilation, for the war at last seemed to be coming to an end. Napoleon had suffered a decisive defeat at the Battle of Leipzig and the British army, under Wellington, had advanced from Spain into South West France. The harvest had been good and trade improved, as European ports once more opened their harbours to British vessels. There was great festivity in London and a mood of optimism swept over the country.

Perhaps Isaac Pocock's play, *The Miller and His Men*, proved so popular when it was first staged at Covent Garden on 21 October because the public were in the mood for something grand and spectacular. With music by Henry Bishop, breath-taking settings, a tremendous explosion at the conclusion, under the overall co-ordination of Charles Farley, who also played the villainous miller, Grindoff, the play could not fail. It was performed over fifty times during the season, became a popular toy theatre play and was frequently revived in the years to come. Liston *Pl. 8* played the principal low comedy role, Karl, a foolish, cowardly servant, who, despite his pert, bumptious manner, helps to bring about the play's happy ending.

Liston played innumerable roles in melodrama, providing comic relief in many a mediocre production. Authors were criticised for lugging Liston into new pieces, such as *The Secret Mine* (1812), in which he played Dimdim, a Chinese slave, merely because they knew his countenance would guarantee a few laughs. Such plays as this or Frederick Reynolds' *The Virgin of the Sun* were more preoccupied with the recreation of violent earthquakes or hurricanes upon the stage, each new production trying to surpass the spectacular effects of the last. When Liston played Blaise, a foolish ostler in *The Forest of Bondy* (1814), Hazlitt noticed that among the dumb-boys, sagacious poodles and cascades of real water, Liston was as usual, "condemned to sustain the Jack-pudding character of the concern". He enjoyed Liston's performance, however, especially "for the oily richness of expression which trickles down this gentleman's face, and makes it shine all over with gladness".[17] Pocock, in particular, wrote buffoon roles for Liston in further melodramas, including Buffardo in *Zembucca* and Mimiski in *John Du Bart*, a play which entailed the appearance on stage of a life-size ship, much to the terror of the audience as it bore down upon them. The parts written for Liston in melodrama are rather like the Idle Jack, Wishee-Washee roles of modern pantomime. This sort of stereotyping was explicitly criticised by the *Examiner*(16/1/ 1814) when it complained:

Last of all in order, but first in importance, thrust into your piece – never mind if he fits his place – a buffoon: dress him like a monster, let him be a drunkard, a coward and a liar, and then make interest with some ingenious humourist to give you a comic song for him to roar, and your work is finished.

If on the stage Liston played the buffoon, in private life he mixed in very different circles. Sometimes, when he had finished performing for the evening, he would walk over to Charles Lamb's home, to attend one of his Wednesday evening suppers. Apart from John Philip Kemble, who occasionally accompanied him, he was the only actor to attend these gatherings, which had commenced in 1801 and were to continue until 1827. A table of cold meat was always waiting, from which guests replenished themselves between games of piquet and whist. The conversation revolved around literature and ideas and here Liston conversed with Hazlitt, Leigh Hunt, Henry Crabb Robinson, William Godwin and Captain Burney. Liston sometimes partnered Lamb at whist and, on one occasion, even agreed to interest himself in a play Lamb had written, *The Pawnbroker's Daughter*, though nothing seems to have come of it.[18] Liston and his wife also used to visit the Godwins regularly: once they unexpectedly called and interrupted Charles and Mary Lamb and the Godwins at a game of rubber. Crabb Robinson joined them after a while and, by midnight, when the party broke up, both Liston and Charles Lamb were the worse for wear after imbibing large quantities of gin and water.[19]

Charles Mathews and his family remained close friends and were frequent dining companions. Liston often visited Mathews' country cottage at Colney Hatch. Ann Mathews recalled how she once caught a peep of Liston playing hide-and-seek in the garden with Mathews' young son. She was greatly amused when he suddenly produced a snuff box and surreptitiously took a pinch of snuff to heighten his enjoyment of the game he was playing.[20] Liston and Mathews were always playing practical jokes on each other and on their fellow-actors. Mathews once had printed a playbill that announced Liston would appear at the Plymouth Theatre in a performance including fire eating, swallowing a live cat, dancing on the slack wire and singing "The Beautiful Maid", while standing on one leg and balancing a coach-wheel on the other.[21]

During the 1814–15 season at Covent Garden Liston's appearances were spasmodic, for he was kept from acting by rheumatism in his hip. He was not the only comic actor to be afflicted by lameness, temporary or otherwise. Munden was a confirmed sufferer from gout, for years only able to perform when the pain was alleviated. Mathews had recently been crippled for life after an accident in which he and Daniel Terry had been tipped from a carriage, while it was travelling at speed. His hip had been broken, leaving him with one leg shorter than the other and a pronounced limp. He was consequently absent from Covent Garden, convalescing from the accident and performing *At Homes* (a one-man show of his devising) in the provinces. When his wife informed him of Liston's complaint, he sent home a new ointment that had been recommended to him and suggested Liston should try some. Liston followed the advice and, the same evening, accompanied by Ann Mathews and by his own wife, went to a Box at Drury Lane. The ointment proved to have a most unpleasant odour. Everyone who came to sit by them was driven away by the smell and several comments were made. Liston, not then recognised so much by the public, found it all highly amusing.[22]

Liston's ill-health continued throughout the season. After he had returned to the stage early in the new year, he was absent for several weeks again. At the end of the season he was too ill to play Trudge in Colman's *Inkle and Yarico* for his benefit and, in *Music Mad*, he was unable to encore one of his songs. Still, there were consolations. A son, John Terry, had been born in 1813, and a daughter, Emma, in 1814. Now that he had a young family to support, he must have been pleased that he continued to receive as much critical acclaim as ever. Although his growing habit of ad-libbing was sternly received in some quarters, his ability to attract the audience's attention without forcing himself upon them was much admired.[23] Leigh Hunt, assessing the talents of actors in 1815, commented:

At the name of Liston we think we see our readers involuntarily smiling and calling up to their minds that face of irresistable drollery, those hopeless airs, those half-conscious, half-unconscious looks of assumption, that exquisite langour of appeal, and all those inimitable, indescribable somethings which hang about the aspect and person of this creature of humour – for this is his proper appellation; he seems to belong and to be made out of humour itself, and not a person assuming particular characters and putting on just as much humour as suits him; he always looks as if he could not help his own drollery; it seems interwoven with all the good-tempered particles of his nature; and for these reasons, one is sometimes in doubt whether to call him an actor at all, and whether the part he pretends to act is not rather a vehicle for Liston than Liston for the part ... he, in a manner, overdoes all characters with an exuberance of personal humour and the audience are still thinking of Liston and content to give up the character, as it were, for his sake. He is decidedly a pet of their own and may be reckoned the most fortunate performer now living.[24]

At the heart of Liston's popularity was his ludicrous face and it was to this feature that he owed much of his success. "This face" commented one critic around this time, "has done a great deal for his fame; and no damsel of romance ever made a greater progress in fortune, and in glory, by her lovely countenance, ·than Mr. Liston made by his grotesque physiognomy". An epigram entitled *Liston's Dream* in the *Theatrical Inquisitor* for September 1813 further demonstrated the importance of Liston's face: *Pl. 14*

> As *Liston* lay wrapt in delicious repose,
> Most harmoniously playing a tune on his nose,
> In a dream there appear'd the adorable *Venus*,
> Who said, "to be sure, there's no likeness between us.
> Yet, to show a *celestial* to kindness so prone is,
> Your looks shall soon rival the handsome *Adonis*".
> Liston woke in a fright and cried, "Heaven Preserve me!"
> If my *face* you *improve*, zounds! madame, *you'll starve me!*"

Not only was Liston dependent on his face: according to Hazlitt, who now considered him "the greatest comic genius of the age",[25] he was so dependent on applause that "he would like to see a small dog wag its tail in approbation".[26] As it happened he got all the applause he desired.

Chapter IV

Farewell to Covent Garden – 1816–1822

Oh, ye scene-shifters, ye scene-painters, ye machinists and dress-makers, ye manufacturers of moon and stars that give no light, ye musical composers, ye men in the orchestra, ye fiddlers and trumpeters and players on the double drum and loud bassoon, rejoice! This is your triumph; it is not ours: and ye full-grown, well-fed, substantial, real fairies ... we shall remember you: we shall believe no more in the existence of your fantastic tribe.[1]

Hazlitt, who wrote these lines, had just been to see a spectacular, musical adaptation of *A Midsummer Night's Dream* at Covent Garden. It was the first in a whole series of adaptations of Shakespearean and other classics by the theatre's musical director, Henry Bishop, and the dramatist Frederick Reynolds. The plays were considerably cut and altered and songs were added quite indiscriminately. Hazlitt considered that, apart from the scenery, Liston as Bottom was the only good thing in the piece. Particularly memorable was the nonchalant and bumptious way in which he accepted the caresses of the fairy queen as merely his due.[2] Sadly, though, the part had been horribly mangled by Reynolds, who trans-formed Bottom into a dull, badly written buffoon role, indistinguishable from a thousand others.

A Midsummer Night's Dream was first revived in January 1816 and, despite the objections of purists, it was successful enough to justify further adaptations. In 1819 *The Comedy of Errors* was turned into a musical extravaganza, with songs lifted from a wide range of Shakespeare's plays. Settings and new scenes were specially introduced to facilitate the singing of such songs as "When Icicles Hang by the Wall" and "Bacchus, Monarch of the Vine". Liston was paired with William Farren, a much drier comedian, who normally specialised in playing old men, as the two Dromios. Leigh Hunt was critical of this, when he went to see the performance:

and we are to believe in the identity of their two servants, Liston and Farren, persons no more resembling each other than moisture and draught, or a bowl of cream and a tobacco pipe, or a plum pudding and a pepper box, or an easy chair and a tall country house stool, or a bill of fare and the payment, or a laughing face and the razor that cuts it. The actors, however, might manage their faces a little better than they do, with whiskers and other disguises; especially the servants, who may caricature their faces more. A paste-board nose would go a long way.[3]

Yet, even though Liston and Farren refused to adopt each other's peculiarities, it did not seem to matter, for the revival proved very popular.

Reynolds was very pleased with the success of his adaptations. They drew good houses and helped him, he said, to pay off his Christmas bills.[4] Within a year he had completed another adaptation – *Twelfth Night* was the victim this time. Liston was to play Sir Andrew Aguecheek, a new role for him. In 1811 he had played Malvolio at Covent Garden and, although some found his performance rather stiff, his friend Crabb Robinson considered it "the perfection of nature and art united".[5] Liston's Sir Andrew provoked mixed reactions: not everyone thought that the change of part was greatly to his advantage. Leigh Hunt felt that Liston was not quite up to the character:

He doted well upon the fool's jokes; but he did not give the other humours in general with sufficient prominence of absurdity, sufficient ostentation and overweeningness.[6]

An exception was his drunkeness in the carousal scene, when, with dimmed eye and trembling feet, he amused the audience by his failure to relight his pipe. The duel scene with Viola was also "ludicrous to perfection". "The faintness with which he sinks back on Sir Toby", commented Hunt, "is absolute dissolution and thaw".[7] Liston went too far for some spectators at this point by climbing halfway up the Covent Garden proscenium arch to demonstrate his fright.

These adaptations were becoming an annual event at Covent Garden and Liston was usually a part of them. In 1821 *The Two Gentlemen of Verona* was revived with Liston as Launce. The production was very spectacular: the settings included marble halls, cooled with water jets, dark woods, shrubbed lawns, torrents, casinos and there was also a magnificent carnival with processions, dances and pageants. The production was so complicated that, occasionally, things went wrong. One evening two wings of the Palace of Hours partly and suddenly disappeared, and a carpenter, who had been trying to put things right, made his debut to the audience in an unwilling somersault over the clouds and remained for some time with his heels kicking in the air. Then the boat, which was to bear the fugitives to Milan, met with so sudden a check that its rower was capsized into the stream. Since his attempts to set the vessel afloat proved hopeless, he just got up and walked off through the waves.[8]

Liston's performance was variously received by the critics. For some reason he used a handsome Newfoundland dog, instead of the filthy cur which is supposed to be Launce's pet dog. He didn't take the performance too seriously. Often, when he came on stage, he would fix his eye on somebody in the pit and so disconcert them that the whole audience would burst out laughing. Every night he would try to make Abbott, the actor playing Valentine, laugh, either by grimacing or snorting. Still, as usual, Liston's presence in the cast had contributed to the play's popularity.

Reynolds did not only ransack the comedies of Shakespeare for his adaptations. Thomas Harris, proprietor of Covent Garden, had suggested to him that Fletcher's *The Humorous Lieutenant* should be restored to the stage, since he felt that it might again become popular with Liston in the title role. So Reynolds set to work on a new adaptation, carefully expunging all references to the venereal disease which provides the Lieutenant's principal motivation. The production, first staged in 1817, was marred by a total misunderstanding of the word "humours" and by Liston's failure to do justice to Fletcher's original creation. Criticised as the "Dull" Lieutenant in some newspapers, the play was withdrawn after only four performances. At least Buckingham's adaptation of Fletcher's *The Chances*, further adapted by Reynolds into *Don Juan* or *The Two Violettas*, did not fare so badly in 1821. Liston played the quarrelsome Fratioso, but turned him into a burlesque character. His comic business in an eating and drinking scene was so outlandish that it seemed more appropriate to Grimaldi in the Christmas Harlequinade. Even worse, when the play was revived for Catherine Stephens' benefit a year later, Charles Kemble as Don Juan had Liston in continuous fits of laughter by tickling him with his sword.[9] Despite (or because of) such horseplay, *Don Juan* avoided the fate of *The Humorous Lieutenant*.

Liston was not totally dependent on Reynolds for the provision of more traditional roles. Some of Shakespeare's plays were lucky enough to escape Reynold's improvements and Liston also played in a number of these. Earlier in his career he had played Polonius and he was quite *Pl. 2(c)* successful as Pompey in *Measure for Measure*. Hazlitt, who saw him play the part in 1816, commented:

M.ᴿ LISTON. ᴀs MOLL FLAGGON.

Plate 9 Liston as Moll Flaggon in *Lord of the Manor*

Scene in the Comic Opera of the LORD of the MANOR, Song Moll Flaggon, Sung by Mʳ Liston.

Plate 10 Scene from *The Lord of the Manor*

BOMBASTES FURIOSO (6).

O! FUSBOS, FUSBOS, I AM DIDDLED QUITE

Plate 11 Scene from *Bombastes Furioso*

Plate 12 Liston as Lubin Log in *Love, Law and Physic*

Plate 13 Scene from *Love, Law and Physic*. "Liston, as Lubin Log, asks the lawyer whether he means to say that 'black is white', and Mathews angrily desires to know if he dares to dispute a point of law with him. The uncertainty, mixed with distrust, in Liston's face, and the assumed obstreperousness, intended to bear down all doubt, in the others, are admirable." Percy Fitzgerald, *The World Behind the Scenes*. The illustration also shows Blanchard as Dr. Camphor and Emery as Andrew

Plate 14 Liston's Dream

Plate 15 Liston as Lord Grizzle in *Epilogue on an Ass*

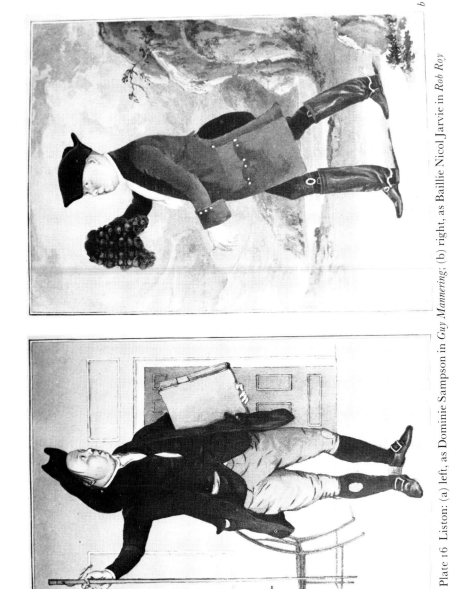

Plate 16 Liston: (a) left, as Dominie Sampson in *Guy Mannering*; (b) right, as Baillie Nicol Jarvie in *Rob Roy*

We cannot say that the Clown Pompey suffered in the hands of Mr. Liston; on the contrary, he played it inimitably well. His manner of saying "a dish of some three-pence" was worth anything. In the scene of his examination before the Justice, he delayed and dallied, and dangled in his answers, in the true spirit of the genius of his author.[10]

He was not so memorable as Cloten, a part that might have seemed perfectly adapted to him. Indeed, if the performance of Shakespeare be the test of a true actor, then Liston would have to be considered deficient. Unlike the tragedians of the day, whose reputations were founded on their interpretations of the classic Shakespeare roles, Liston depended for his success on the creation of new, original roles. In parts especially written for him he was fine, but, in Shakespeare, he seems to have used the roles merely as an excuse for buffoonery and low comedy. This was not altogether his fault: he was merely conforming to the practice of presenting Shakespearian comedy in the style of contemporary melodrama, in which spectacle, music and low comedy were the predominant features.

This tendency emerged in another development at Covent Garden, with which Liston was also associated. Walter Scott had recently begun to publish anonymously the Waverley novels. These were not only very popular with the reading public, but also on the stage, where they allowed for the introduction of spectacular scenery, music, melodramatic incident and diverse, but strongly drawn, characters. Most theatres hastened to present dramatisations of the novels as soon as they were issued and often several versions would run concurrently. Liston was closely involved with some of these productions and recreated several of Scott's most successful characters upon the stage.

Two months after he had performed Bottom in 1816, Liston appeared before the public as Dominie Sampson in Daniel Terry's adaptation of *Guy Mannering*. Liston's performance as the kindly, absent-minded tutor, with his catchphrase of "Prodigious!" every time he is startled by some new and unexpected event, proved very memorable. Hazlitt admired "the unconscious simplicity of his humour[11] and considered it "one of the finest pieces of acting on the stage, both for humour and feeling, invention and expression".[12] "By the way", wrote Scott to Terry, "Liston's Dominie is a very fine thing and does him infinite credit".[13] Liston so successfully combined comedy and pathos in his interpretation, especially when he refused the offer of money from Lucy Bertram, who can no longer afford to pay for his services as tutor, that he drew tears from his audience. According to George Daniel, the enterprising editor of Cumberland's British Theatre:

Pl. 16(a)

Liston's Dominie Sampson was unique – a rare union of the pathetic and humorous, indeed we are not sure that the tears did not out-number the smiles. Liston draw tears? Contemplate that richly comic physiognomy! Listen to those unctuous tones! Mark that indescribable by-play! – in a word, look at Liston from top to toe and believe it if you can. Those who had the good fortune to see this marvellous perform-ance will confirm our assertions – Liston drew abundant tears, provok'd gentle smiles and commanded universal respect and attention, and made the theatre ring with laughter.[14]

Not surprisingly, the Dominie proved one of Liston's most popular roles in the years to come.

However, even though Liston drew tears in his performance, he was occasionally accused of "gagging", the practice of interpolating lines or business to disconcert his fellow performers, as well. Lord William Lennox, whose penchant for pretty young actresses made him a frequent visitor before and behind the scenes, complained that Liston's object, in the early part of the play, was to get a smile from Catherine Stephens, as Lucy Bertram, at the height of her grief, and that he usually succeeded.[15] In time other touches were added, which had nothing to do with the play itself. After the curtain had closed on the final scene, Liston would remain in front of it in a brown study and look distractedly around him, exclaiming "Prodigious!" Occasionally he would time his exit so as to meet Abbott – the Colonel Mannering of the evening – coming on to announce the play for the following night, when considerable horseplay would take place between them. This was no accidental occurrence, but carefully arranged in the green-room beforehand.

Pl. 16(b)   Two years later Liston brought to life another Scott original, Baillie Nicol Jarvie in *Rob Roy MacGregor*. Catherine Stephens played Diana Vernon and William Macready was Rob Roy in this adaptation, which had been competently executed by Isaac Pocock. Liston's dry humour and ludicrous gravity provided a very convincing portrait of the Glasgow merchant, although some were annoyed by the "sawney, ridiculous faces he pulled"[16], particularly whilst Catherine Stephens was singing the ballad of "Aud Lang Syne". "In the skirmish scene", wrote the *Theatrical Inquisitor* (March, 1818), "we almost fancied ourself in the highland pass, surrounded by the characters of the novelist. Liston painted the terrors of the Glasgow merchant admirably well". Although his Baillie may have been a little broader than Scott intended and even though his catch-phrase, "My conscience!" was an interpolation, Liston succeeded in bringing the character to life and continued to play the role for more than a decade.

He was less successful in some of the other Scott characters he undertook. As Dumbiedikes in *The Heart of Mid-Lothian* (1819), another of Terry's adaptations, he was totally unmemorable. Ironically, Scott had previously written to Terry that much would depend upon Dumbiedikes, "in which Liston will be strong".[17] As Jonathan Oldbuck in *The Antiquary* he was indifferent and for once failed to render a character amusing. After Pocock's version of the novel had proved unsuccessful in 1818, Terry re-adapted it in 1820: Liston apart, this version was popular, for it included a duel, a dramatic rescue during a storm and some ballads sweetly sung by Catherine Stephens. Shortly after he appeared in the 1820 *Antiquary*, Liston played Wamba the jester in *Ivanhoe*, again with little effect. It was not until 1822, when he played Captain Dalgetty in Pocock's adaptation of *Montrose*, that he again made a Scott character especially his own.

Montrose was staged most spectacularly and no effort was spared in this production. It commenced with the landscape and horizon gradually appearing out of a rising mist, which was so convincing that one old gentleman in the pit begged his daughter to put her handkerchief to her mouth and take care of her cough.[18] The children of the mist, who were also gradually revealed, were less convincing. Ranged about in a stiff and formal manner, they displayed more anxiety about the size of the audience than about the imminent return of their chief. Liston played Captain Dalgetty with fearless good nature and displayed excellent horsemanship in what was considered one of the best representations of the general havoc of foot and horse action then exhibited upon the stage. However, perhaps because of the immense difficulties involved in staging it, *Montrose* was not revived again after this season.

The works of Scott and Shakespeare did not provide the only sources for adaptation at Covent Garden during these years. Henry Bishop decided that it would also be feasible to adapt the operas of Mozart and Rossini in order to make their music accessible to a wider public. To this end he added music of his own and any popular ballad then current in order to make the scores a little easier to follow. In 1817 *Don Giovanni* was transformed into *The Libertine*, with Charles Kemble as the Don. As Kemble could not sing very well, most of his arias were transferred to Masetto. Liston was Leporello, which he played in a mixed style, partly as a burlesque imitation of the Italian Opera, partly as himself. He lacked a sufficiently strong voice for the part, but he seems to have brought out its comedy.

In October, 1818, Liston played Figaro in *The Barber of Seville*. Again he bravely sang the role, which was more than could be said of Count Almaviva, who expediently made use of an attendant to do all his singing for him. Liston made the character laughable, despite the poorness of the translation, and was comical in the shaving scene. The bustling, intriguing Figaro does not seem a typical Liston part, yet six months later he was again playing the comic servant, this time in *The Marriage of Figaro*. Most reviewers found Liston an amusing and adequate Figaro in this production, except for the *Theatrical Inquisitor*:

> The character of Figaro – it complained – was totally lost in every respect, both in mirth and in music, which was precisely the case in *The Barber of Seville*. Mr. Bishop seems to have no notion of this character; indeed, assignment of it to Mr. Liston renders it impossible that the public should know anything about it either. Figaro is not a buffoon; his merit with his master does not consist in making faces, nor saying funny things, but in a spirit of vivacious intrigue, which made him enter, *con amore*, into plots to obtain Susanna, and with equal alertness to counteract them, when directed against his choice. For Mr. Liston to attempt Mozart's music seems to us little short of sacrilege.[19]

Whatever the shortcomings of Liston's singing or interpretation, he appeared frequently in revivals of these operas and was the first actor to sing Figaro and Leporello in English.

During the 1816–17 Covent Garden season, when he first played Leporello, Liston also scored a hit as the cockney Fogrun in Thomas Morton's *The Slave*. One June day in 1817 the following letter appeared in a number of London newspapers, referring to these two roles:

> Sir,
>
> My benefit takes place this evening at Covent Garden Theatre, and I doubt not, will be splendidly attended. Several parties in the first circle of fashion were made, the moment it was announced. I shall perform Fogrun in *The Slave* and Leporello in *The Libertine*; and in the delineation of these arduous characters, I shall display much feeling and discrimination together with great taste in my dresses and elegance in my manner. The audience will be delighted by my exertions and testify by rapturous applause, their most decided approbation.
>
> When we consider in addition to my professional merits the loveliness of my person and the fascination of my face, which are only equalled by the amicability of my private character, having "never pinched my children nor kicked my wife out of bed", there is no doubt but this puff will not be exerted in vain,
>
> I am, sir, your obedient servant,
> John Liston.[20]

The "puff" certainly paid off, for Liston drew "a tolerably good house"[21] for this programme.

Benefits, by which actors took a share of the profits after the everyday expenses of the theatre had been allowed for, were a lucrative means of increasing one's income, in London and the provinces. A popular actor could, with a well chosen programme of entertainments, make several hundred pounds from a good benefit. Liston took great pains in selecting material for his benefits and usually attracted large audiences. Sometimes he would exploit personal successes: after he had first played in *Guy Mannering*, he introduced a new song at his benefit, *Dominie Sampson in Love, Prodigious!* His Covent Garden benefit for 1818 was especially notorious. Not long before he had read a memoir of the Restoration comedian, Jo Haines. An epilogue Haines had once spoken, whilst riding on an ass, had created such mirth, that he had spent a full half-an-hour speaking it. A footnote had contained the comment "a hint to Liston"[22] and Liston took up the hint. He asked old Lowndes, the bookseller, to find him a copy of the epilogue, but when he read it, he was not too sure it would work. So he asked Colman to rewrite it for him, to be delivered in the character of Lord Grizzle. Colman obliged and, when Liston performed it for the first time, with the opening lines:

> Behold the pair of us! before the curtain,
> A prettier couple can't be found, that's certain

it was rapturously received and encored by the audience. They were especially amused when Liston recommended the ass as a fit candidate at the ensuing general election. However, Liston had scarcely begun the Epilogue for a second time, when he was reduced to silence by a most untoward event. The ass suddenly relieved itself, rather brazenly, on stage. The audience burst into loud laughter and all was confusion for some time. A Bath clergyman, John Genest, was sitting in one of the side boxes and saw plainly what the ass was about to do. He thought that if any other person had seen from the side-screens and had called to Liston, the castastrophe might have been averted.[23]

Pl. 15

As the years passed by Liston found that he was kept very busy at Covent Garden, for the Management could hardly do without him. England might be in recession, on account of post-war inflation; rumblings of discontent might be arising in rural and industrial areas; but at Covent Garden Liston continued to relieve the cares and worries of his London audience. However dreadful the times, he was always there, ready to offer a couple of hours of laughter and respite. His popularity was surprising, considering the mediocrity of some of the new roles with which he was provided. A few, such as Fogrun, Jocrisse in Morton's *Henri Quatre* or Pengoose in Colman's *The Law of Java* were quite successful, but too many of the parts were either underwritten or otherwise hollow imitations of old favourites like Lubin Log. Even the combination of Liston and Grimaldi in *The Marquis de Carabas*, a version of *Puss-in-Boots*, failed because of the poor quality of the script. In general, though, the Covent Garden Management knew that, if they announced in their playbills that a new character would be undertaken by Liston, then there was a strong guarantee of good attendance.

In many ways Covent Garden made inadequate use of its comic performers during these years. Mathews left the company, partly because of his lameness, partly because he was disgusted at the sort of parts he was expected to play.[24] The actors were often allowed insufficient time for rehearsal: a new farce was read in the green-room one day, rehearsed the next and performed the day after.[25] In such circumstances Liston was not used to great advantage in many of the comedies and farces bolstered up by his presence. Many of these lasted only two or three nights, redeemed alone by the quality of Liston's performance. He was paid £17 a week for his services, then the principal salary paid to a comic performer at Covent Garden,[26] even though his value to the theatre was much greater. The proud, gentlemanly comedian, forced to play the most ephemeral and unmemorable of parts, found the situation increasingly untenable.

Liston was luckier in the farces and comedies that the Haymarket Theatre provided for him. He rejoined the company in 1818 and again became the mainstay of most of their summer seasons. The dissension between Morris and Colman was over, with Morris victorious. Liston was consequently able to settle into a series of secure engagements, delighting audiences by performing old favourites and by creating new roles. Hazlitt was particularly struck by Sir Peter Pigwiggin in *Pigeons and Crows*, a new comedy by Thomas Moncrieff, first performed in 1819:

> What a name, what a person! and what a representative! We never saw Mr. Liston's countenance in better preservation; that is, it seems tumbling all in pieces with indescribable emotions, and a thousand odd twitches, and unaccountable absurdities, oozing out at every pore. His jaws seem to ache with laughter: his eyes look out of his head with wonder: his face is unctuous all over and bathed with jests; the top of his nose is tickled with conceit of himself, and his teeth chatter in his head in the eager insinuation of a plot: his forehead speaks, and his wig (not every particular hair, but the whole bewildered bushy mass), stands on end as life were in it.[27]

The following year was to be the last in the little theatre, for there were plans to construct a new theatre slightly to the south, designed externally by the architect Nash. A strong company had been engaged, again with Liston as its pivot. A newcomer to the company was Madame Eliza Vestris, a vivacious and very attractive young actress, then in her early twenties. Dark-haired, with large lustrous eyes, she was rapidly becoming a favourite with the public and, in the years to come, her career was to be quite closely linked with Liston's.

Liston's major hit during the season was Sam Swipes, a vulgar cockney pot-boy in *Exchange no Robbery*. Theodore Hook was the author – he had loosely adapted it from an eighteenth century play, *He Would be a Soldier* – but his circumstances were then too equivocal to allow him to own to the authorship. He had recently returned in disgrace from a colonial appointment as Governor of Mauritius. Serious irregularities were discovered and he was prosecuted by the Government for a claim of £12,000 and imprisoned. It was later discovered that the money had been embezzled by a subordinate and that Hook was merely chargeable with gross neglect of duty. He was released, but the charges against him were not rescinded. He returned to writing – both plays and novels – and became editor of *John Bull*. He remained improvident and his difficulties finally broke him in health and spirit.

Sam Swipes, with his urchin hair-cut and innate vulgarity was a perfect copy of "the human animal in its most debased and vulgar state".[28] *Pl. 18* Mistaken as the heir to a baronetcy and restored to his supposed father he adopts the outward appearance of a gentleman, but retains the manners and inclinations of a pot-boy. Dressed in the extreme of fashion, except for his hair, which remains distinctly plebeian, he prefers to frequent the servants' quarters and hankers after his former sweetheart, Polly Watts. Sam Swipes was only conceivable, claimed George Daniel, when associated with Liston's particular style of acting.[29] His unpolished manner, awkward gait, and outrageous appearance contributed to one of his most original creations since Lubin Log.

Liston's performance of characters like Sam Swipes was effective because of the detailed observation he put into them. He created on stage as rich a gallery of characters as Dickens was later to create in his novels. He was as much an author as an actor, fleshing out the most underwritten parts with his creative genius. His vitality on stage must have resembled the vitality with which Dickens described some of his more eccentric characters in his novels.[30] So convincing were some of Liston's impersonations that he left his audience very uncomfortable. Playgoers like William Robson didn't know whether to laugh or feel sorry for characters as ignorant and unthinking as Sam Swipes.[31] There was something pathetic about such creatures, even if the audiences could feel complacent about their exemption from such foibles. Petty, greedy, ignorant, small-minded, many of Liston's characters would have been most unattractive in real life. On stage, however, they seemed to provide an endless fund of amusement.

When not performing at the Haymarket or Covent Garden, Liston continued to extend the range of his provincial engagements. To Newcastle and Liverpool he added Edinburgh, Bath, Dublin and the Midlands as suitable venues for his provincial tours. In 1816, in company with Charles Mathews, he visited Dublin and the following spring he made his debut at Edinburgh. Sir Walter Scott went to see him play Dominie Sampson while he was there and managed to see Liston for a few minutes behind the scenes.[32] During the summer he visited Liverpool and Birmingham and then, in December 1818, he "conquered all present"[33] at the Brighton Theatre. At Bath, where he performed during April, 1821, he was considered one of the greatest attractions ever to appear there. John Genest met Liston during this engagement and was amused by some of the anecdotes that Liston related. He told Genest that he had determined never to play Lord Grizzle outside London, after an unfortunate experience in a provincial theatre. One night T. P. Cooke, who was playing Glumdalca, had fastened a large bladder behind himself. When he died there was a loud explosion and incessant peals of laughter from the audience. This so disconcerted Liston, he found he could do nothing more with his own part.[34]

Often, when he toured the provinces, Liston was joined by his wife, who would appear during his benefit performance at the end of the engagement. He was not happy, though, about her remaining on the stage. Now that there was a young family to look after and his earning power was so high, he encouraged her to retire, following in the footsteps of Ann Mathews, who had left the stage some years before. They therefore announced that, at her Covent Garden benefit for 1822, Mrs. Liston would make her last appearance on any stage. Liston also announced his intention of leaving Covent Garden that summer, since his contract was due to expire. He was now aware that he could make a greater profit from provincial engagements than from the relatively meagre salary paid him at Covent Garden. He would have more freedom over the parts he played and he would no longer be restricted over the nature of his summer engagements outside Covent Garden, as he had been over his contract with the English Opera House. Also, since Covent Garden now seemed to be in the grip of economic difficulties, he would avoid the sort of dangers caused by the theatre's unstable financial state as well.

Liston probably made his decision to leave Covent Garden before he knew that his good friend Charles Kemble had been appointed the new manager. Although Kemble told him that he did not want to lose him at any cost,[35] Liston was adamant about going. Liston had already negotiated a number of provincial engagements for the forthcoming season, although it was rather a shock to Kemble when he discovered that Liston had signed articles with Drury Lane on 2 September to appear there the following year. Kemble had already been embroiled in a salary dispute with Catherine Stephens and Charles Young, the tragedian. Still on fixed salaries, they realised that their worth to the theatre was greatly in excess of the salaries they received. Their demands, with which Liston became associated, helped to inaugurate the "star" system. And, while Covent Garden was intransigent, Drury Lane proved more flexible. At the time there was an informal agreement between the managers of the two theatres that neither would sign up performers from the other house until a period of one year had elapsed between the old and new engagement. Robert William Elliston, flamboyant actor-manager of Drury Lane, appropriately enough known as the Great Lessee, ignored the agreement and engaged Young, Liston and Catherine Stephens for the forthcoming season. If his conduct was unprincipled, his business acumen was strong. He offered them more than twice the salaries they were receiving at Covent Garden, but limited to fixed-term engagements, which allowed the actors greater freedom and were not too financially crippling for the management.

Since his meteoric debut in January 1814, Kean had been the sole support of Drury Lane. His volatile, passionate performances of the great Shakespearian roles had wooed the audiences and delighted Hazlitt, who had championed him ever since he first appeared at Drury Lane, one cold winter night, as Shylock. With Elliston's engagement of the Covent Garden defectors, Kean's supremacy was over, a fact to which he did not take kindly. At first he refused to act with Charles Young, but eventually he conceded. His position as first tragedian remained uncontested, although the 1820s were to see a decline in his health, powers and popularity. By the middle of that decade Hazlitt's other favourite, Liston, was to prove even more of a draw than Kean.

For Covent Garden an era had ended. Three of their principal performers had left to go to another theatre. Then, in the summer of 1822, John Emery died, after bursting a blood vessel in his lungs – he had been a heavy drinker and his fondness for brandy proved his undoing. He left behind not only a wife and several children, but also two dependent parents as well. William Macready did not stay at Covent Garden very much longer: he found it a "desert"[36] on his return in autumn 1822 and engaged at Drury Lane the following season. Henry Bishop, who had contributed so much to the musical prowess of the theatre, also departed in 1823, after a claim for a rise in salary was disputed by the Management.

For his last benefit at Covent Garden Liston played Shelty in O'Keeffe's *The Highland Reel* and Sir Bashful Constant in Murphy's *The Way to Keep Him*. Between the two comedies Sarah Liston came forward and sang her *Valedictory Address*, which Colman had written especially for her. She expressed all the feelings natural to such an occasion and the audience warmly paid tribute to all the delight she had given them in the past. A short, dumpling, fair-complexioned figure, she stood on the Covent

Pl. 4(b) Garden stage, looking, as one joker put it, "like a fillet of veal upon castors".[37] Then, the farewells over, she took her bow and retired. Another successful benefit was over, as were seventeen years professional and social association with Covent Garden Theatre.

Liston's departure from Covent Garden gave rise to rumours that he was leaving the stage, as he was heir to a baronetcy.[38] In fact, even if his aloof, enigmatic personality fuelled such rumours, retirement was far from his intentions and he remained as busy as ever. He went straight to the Haymarket Theatre, where he remained until October, and then set off on a gruelling provincial tour, which included Cheltenham, Birmingham and Liverpool. He was again engaged at the Dublin Theatre, where, on 14 December, he witnessed a minor riot. The Lord Lieutenant, the Marquis of Wellesley, was visiting the theatre that night. He had recently banned the Orange body from their customary celebration of the landing of William III in England. During the first play, *She Stoops to Conquer*, there were cries of "No Popery" and "Groan for the Lord Mayor". Order was restored, but when Liston as Tony Lumpkin and Williams as Hardcastle appeared, carrying silver tankards, they were called upon by some of the audience to drink "the pious, glorious and immortal memory". They refused to do this, and the disturbance continued. During the fourth act a placard was thrown at the Lord Lieutenant and, during the fifth, a disturbance broke out in the gallery. The National Anthem was hurriedly played, in the hope that this would restore order. Cries then arose for Boyne water and a bottle, hurled at the Lord Lieutenant's box, hit the drop scene with much force. In the next piece, *Tom Thumb*, just as Liston entered as Lord Grizzle, a piece of wood, part of a rattle, hit the stage box. Liston bowed and retired.[39] He was much relieved to return to England where, after Christmas and a short engagement at the Manchester Theatre, he would soon be making his debut at Drury Lane.

Chapter V

Drury Lane Debut – 1823–1825

Liston was nervous, as frightened as any new apprentice.[1] The day had been fraught with difficulties. The playbills announced that he would appear for the first time at the Drury Lane Theatre on 28 January, 1823, as Tony Lumpkin in *She Stoops to Conquer*. But the weather was poor and it was unlikely that a large audience would venture out in such inclement conditions. Earlier in the day Munden had sent word to the theatre to say that he would be unable to play Hardcastle that night, as his gout was playing him up. Liston was on good terms with Munden, but it is likely that the veteran actor was not too happy about Liston usurping his territory at Drury Lane. Another problem was the new environment itself: unlike Covent Garden Drury Lane was less well-organised behind the scenes and the tone of the green-room was not so civilised. Still, his anxiety was slightly relieved by the sparkling company of Charles Mathews' son at dinner[2] and, in the event, he need not have worried. An enthusiastic audience turned out to welcome him back to London and he delighted them all with his portrait of Tony's booby imbecility. *Pl. 17*

Engaged at £50 per week,[3] Liston was now free to concentrate upon the revival of old favourites and the creation of new roles especially written for him. He joined a corps of comic actors perhaps even stronger than Covent Garden had once boasted. Not only was Munden engaged there, as strong as ever in his established parts, but also William Dowton, especially acclaimed for his Falstaff, his Sir Antony Absolute and his Dr. Cantwell in *The Hypocrite*: both provided a link with the comic tradition of the late eighteenth century. In parts requiring high spirits, including those that Mathews had played, was John Pritt Harley, an actor of growing popularity. Edward Knight, commonly known as "little" Knight, played the countrymen. Even the manager, Elliston, occasionally played in comedy. Tragedy and song were also well represented, since Kean, Young, Catherine Stephens and John Braham were all members of Elliston's star-studded company.

45

Liston was soon performing his most popular roles at Drury Lane, including Sam Swipes and Apollo Belvi in *Killing No Murder*. Harley took over Buskin, Mathews' old role, and on the first night of the revival cut off two of Liston's lines in the duet. Liston, although not completely at home in his new surroundings, was not prepared to be cut off at all. He put out his hand and looked at Harley as if to say, "Have you a heart hard enough to do this?" Harley stopped immediately and bowed apologetically to Liston, much to the audience's amusement. A greater difficulty arose when Liston was announced to play Lubin Log in *Love, Law and Physic*. A letter arrived from Covent Garden shortly before the play was to be performed, informing Drury Lane that the play was the property of Covent Garden and could not be performed elsewhere.[4] Drury Lane ignored this letter; sensibly, for Lubin Log was one of Liston's best roles and virtually unactable by anyone else.

Only once did Liston play opposite Edmund Kean, as Launcelot Gobbo to Kean's Shylock in *The Merchant of Venice*. Although this rich combination of talent was quite successful, they appeared in no other plays together. Liston, so the story goes, laid a wager with Kean (who said that nothing could disturb his seriousness while on stage) that he could succeed in making him laugh even there. Once, when Kean was playing Rolla, a procession of veiled virgins of the sun had to enter and pass before him. The first virgin, as she passed, suddenly raised her veil, confronted Kean with the ludicrous face of Liston and the wager was won, for Kean went off into an uncontrollable fit of laughter.[5] Kean was very conscious of his status as a tragic actor and, on the whole, did not take kindly to the fact that Liston could vie with him in income, status or popularity. When he was asked to act one Monday evening, because it was doubtful whether Liston would be available, he refused, saying that he would not be made a stop gap to the property he had been so long supporting. A few years later, when he returned unexpectedly to Drury Lane one evening, he flew into a terrible rage because Liston's things were in his dressing room, evidently furious that a mere comic actor should be allowed to use it.[6]

Liston's transfer to Drury Lane was quickly proving a great success. Figaro, Baillie Jarvie and Dominie Sampson were among the old favourites that he played once more, though he created some new roles as well. Most successful of these was Tristram Sappy, "a guzzling, stupid, economical idiot", in John Poole's *Deaf as a Post*. Although not well received on its first performance, the play soon caught on and Sappy, quite an old part under a new name, became another popular Liston role. His selfishness, in quibbling over the cost of a tavern bill, and his consternation during a supper scene, in which dish after dish is snatched away from under his nose, provided another carefully observed portrayal

Pl. 19

of human weakness and stupidity. Not surprisingly, when Liston went off to Edinburgh and Glasgow in March, to fulfil some previously contracted engagements, Drury Lane speedily wrote to him, requesting his return. In his businesslike way, Liston politely wrote back to say that he could not break off his commitments in Scotland prematurely, but that he would be back at his post as soon as possible. He had forgotten, when he made the Drury Lane engagement, that he had agreed to play for twelve rather than six days in Edinburgh. Drury Lane had suggested that, since he would be returning a week later than expected, he might play a week for them gratis. Liston wrote back to say that he had not taken any notice of this suggestion, but that it was a very good joke.[7] Back in London he continued to draw large audiences and, although it began to rain just as the doors of the theatre opened, he even drew a big crowd for his benefit performance.

Liston spent the summer season at the Haymarket Theatre, where his success continued unabated. He gave an especially superb performance as the love-lorn cockney waiter, Billy Lackaday, in James Kenney's new comic opera, *Sweethearts and Wives*, first performed on 7 July. Tearful, *Pl. 20* despairing, Liston's whole appearance was that of sea-sickness, with his heart in his mouth and his eyes rolling in his head. Pathos and absurdity combined in "this ludicrous compound of love, imbecility and shrewdness".[8] His song, with its refrain

> Oh Lackaday,
> Pity Billy Lackaday!

was, according to Crabb Robinson, "the perfection of farce".[9] Every time Liston appeared on stage, the audience was convulsed with laughter. Indeed, so successful was this new piece that it completely overshadowed the other Haymarket productions of that year and was repeated over fifty times.

About two months after the play had been first performed, something strange happened. The overture to the play had just ended when, suddenly, the orchestra struck up and played it all over again. The audience began to grow impatient and one of the actors, Vining, appeared to explain that the delay was caused by the unexpected absence of Mr. Liston. The audience was not satisfied and called for the manager. Daniel Terry now came forward on his behalf and told them that it was quite unprecedented for Mr. Liston not to be punctual, and no doubt he would be present in a few minutes, if no accident had occurred to him. The piece then commenced and, at the appropriate moment, Liston entered with book in hand and advanced to the front of the stage, to address the audience:

Ladies and Gentlemen, (he said) I trust you will grant me your indulgence, as I hope you are aware of my customary attention to my duty. I can assure you that it was not my fault – I was deceived myself; being informed that the first piece would take an hour and a quarter, which has not proved the case, and therefore I could not help it, and I hope you will excuse me.

Liston was loudly applauded and, when he resumed his role, his usual expression of "This comes of reading novels" vastly amused the audience, who applied it to the circumstances of that evening.[10]

Back at Drury Lane Liston continued to draw large audiences during the 1823–24 season. On the evening of December 1st George IV visited the theatre. He was a great admirer of Liston and commanded performances of *The Hypocrite* and *Love, Law and Physic*, in both of which Liston appeared. His interest in Liston made the actor even more popular and fashionable than he was already. He delighted in Liston's performances: his sides would shake with laughter and tears of mirth used to course down his cheeks. As a mark of his esteem he actually sent Liston an entrée for himself and his friends to his Pavilion at Brighton.[11] On the night in question he arrived in the royal box, surrounded as usual by beefeaters, and took his accustomed seat, with officers of state behind him. William Thackeray was a member of that audience, which he later described in *Vanity Fair*:

How we sang God save him! How the house rocked and shouted with that magnificent music! How they cheered, cried and waved handkerchiefs. Ladies wept; mothers clasped their children: some fainted with emotion. People were suffocated in the pit, shrieks and groans rising up amidst the writing and shouting mass there of his people . . .

George IV had at last been crowned King in 1821 and, after a period of unpopularity caused by his separation from Queen Caroline, he had began to venture into public places once more. At Covent Garden he had recently laughed so much at Grimaldi's jokes that he had burst his stays. Now "florid of face, portly of person, covered in orders, and in a rich curling head of hair",[12] he sat expectantly awaiting the performance of *The Hypocrite*, Isaac Bickerstaffe's eighteenth century adaptation of Moliere's *Tartuffe* and Cibber's *The Non-Juror*. The major part of Dr. Cantwell was played by William Dowton, in a performance so convincingly unctuous that it was almost unpleasant to watch it. Liston played Mawworm, a minor part, but in his hands it became one of the highlights of the play. Mawworm is an ignorant and fanatical preacher and Liston

Pl. 22

based his interpretation on Edward Irving, a well-known evangelical minister who had originally hailed from Scotland. His imitation gave piquancy to his performance throughout the 1820s, although Irving himself was eventually expelled from the pulpit of the little chapel in Hatton Gardens, where he preached, because of his excesses.[13]

The highlight of the play was a sermon which Mawworm delivered at its conclusion from behind a temporary pulpit improvised out of a clothes horse and a table cloth. He informed the assembled company that he alone would be saved and that, as they clung to the tails of his coat, he would fling them off, for he would wear a spencer. The spencer was a garment that had come into fashion in the early part of the century and covered only the top half of the body. The sermon was a fairly recent addition to the play: it had originated in 1809 from Charles Mathews, who felt dissatisfied with the limited opportunities offered by the part. Liston had begun to play Mawworm after Mathews had more-or-less resigned the part on account of his lameness and, with the help of the sermon, he made the part something specially his own.[14]

No sooner did Liston walk on stage on the night of December 1st, with his goggle eyes and lank, carroty locks, when the King, who had been unprepared for anything quite so droll, took measure of the actor, then threw himself back in his chair and roared and rolled with laughter. His mirth infected the whole theatre and when Liston spoke the sermon, there were cries for an encore, the King included. Liston remounted the pulpit, with a shake of his hand at the King's profanity, and started the sermon all over again. The King's response started a fashion for the play and, in particular, for Mawworm's sermon, which was now regularly encored. This was unusual for spoken dialogue and had only happened previously with Emery's jealous scene as Fixture in A Roland for an Oliver. Suddenly, The Hypocrite, which had been a standard part of the theatre's repertory for many years, became the hit of the season. Not only was it fashionable at Drury Lane: many provincial theatres revived it as well during 1824.

When Liston visited Bath and Bristol early in the new year, he was naturally called upon to perform Mawworm. John Genest, who saw him play the role in Bath, felt that he was no better than Mathews in the part. Nor was he very impressed with Liston's first attempt as Lucio in Measure for Measure later in the year at Drury Lane, feeling that Liston was worse than lost in the part.[15] Although he was amusing enough for some critics, Liston lost the character's petulance and was less effective than when he had played Pompey.

Towards the conclusion of the season Joseph Munden came to prominence again, for he was taking his leave of the public in a series of farewell performances. Born in 1758, the son of a Holborn poulterer, Munden fled his early employments as an apothecary's apprentice and as a stationer's clerk to become a strolling player. He eventually became a shareholder in a circuit of theatres that included both Newcastle and Chester, but sold his shares in 1790 when he was invited to Covent Garden to replace the comedian John Edwin, who had recently died. Within two years he had made a spectacular hit in the role of Old Dornton in Holcroft's play *The Road to Ruin* and he stayed with Covent Garden until 1811, when he quit after a salary dispute. He was indignant at the fact that Covent Garden refused to pay him his full salary during a prolonged absence when he was suffering from gout. He transferred to Drury Lane, where he remained until his retirement.

As an actor Munden's distinct characteristic was the continual mobility and distortion of his facial expression. Some critics condemned this as mere buffoonery and grimace: others found it a valid, amusing method of performing. His voice was just as useful an asset: he could put such unusual emphasis upon words that he actually seemed to suggest their physical characteristics. His style of speech was blustering, diffuse, as if he was short of breath or searching for words. Such a mode of speech naturally fitted the volatile, eccentric, blustering middle-aged men he so often played. At his best he could tone down the comedy with pathos, if the part demanded it. He was very good at drunken parts – once he played three drunken characters on the same night and made each of them seem different – and he excelled in playing old men. He was much admired by his contemporaries, particularly Charles Lamb, who left several glowing portraits of him.

Although Liston was a great admirer of Munden's acting and an amicable social relationship existed between them, he did not appear in Munden's farewell benefit on 31 May, 1824. Still, he had been able to help out in an emergency a couple of weeks earlier. On Saturday 15 May Munden was advertised to play Old Rapid in Morton's *A Cure for the Heartache*. This was to be his last performance in the role, but at about 1.30 on the day Munden was led into the green-room looking very ill. He lay on a couch in Kean's corner of the room and was presently seized with violent spasms, the result of a cold he had caught. At 4 p.m. he was taken home by coach and, to appease a disappointed audience, Liston took over his role.[16]

Munden recovered in time for his farewell benefit, when he played Sir Robert Bramble in Colman's *The Poor Gentleman* and Old Dozey in Dibdin's *Past Ten O'Clock and a Rainy Night*. When he appeared before a house crammed with people from the swing door of the pit to the back of the gallery, his reception was deafening: hats and handkerchiefs were waved in the air; sticks beaten; there was loud cheering and applause. He

Plate 17 Liston as Tony Lumpkin *She Stoops to Conquer*

Plate 18 Liston as Sam Swipes in *Exchange No Robbery*

Mᴿ LISTON ᴀs TRISTRAM SAPPY

in Deaf as a Post.

"Let me see, what was I going to say"

Plate 19 Liston as Tristram Sappy in *Deaf as a Post*

MR LISTON
OR
'Billy Lackaday' in 'Sweethearts & Wives'
. . . At [illegible] at the [illegible] Office 310 Strand

Plate 20 Liston as Billy Lackaday in *Sweethearts and Wives*

MR LISTON.

as Van Dunder in 'Twould puzzle a Conjuror.

"Read it indeed! that's very easily said, read it!!"

Plate 21 Liston as Van Dunder in *'Twould Puzzle a Conjuror*

MR LISTON, AS MAW-WORM.

IN THE PLAY OF THE HYPOCRITE ACT 5TH SCENE LAST.

Stay stay you infatuated wretches, you know not what ye do the Doctor is innocent. I say he is
innocent, touch not a hair of his precious head, rumple not one curl of his gracious wig, he's a Saint
if ever there was a Saint he is one, but ye will be the sufferers, I have one great & glorious consolation, I say
one glorious consolation, you'd all go to the D l. I shall go up but you'll go down, and when you see me
mount & have ye to your fate you'll want my aid, you'll want me to take you with me, you'll cling to me
you'll attempt to lay hold of the skirts of my coat, but I'll fling ye all, for I'll war a surtout.

Plate 22 Liston as Maw-worm in *The Hypocrite*

Plate 23 Liston as A Broom Girl

Plate 24 Liston as Simon Pengander in *'Twixt the Cup and the Lip*

advanced to the stage lights, bowed repeatedly and placed his hand on his heart; he was moved to tears and, even when the applause had subsided, he was unable to recollect himself for some time. As Dozey he gave one of his finest performances. In the tavern scene he toasted the health of "old Joe Munden's friends" and was greatly applauded. At the end of the farce he came forward and, in Lamb's view, unwisely read his farewell speech:

> He stammered, and he pressed his heart, – and put on his spectacles, – and blundered his written gratitudes, – and wiped his eyes, and bowed – and stood, – and at last staggered away for ever! The plan of his farewell was bad, but the long life of excellence which really made his farewell pathetic, overcame all defects, and the people and Joe Munden parted like lovers![17]

Munden lived on for another eight years, in a state of poverty that could easily have been rectified if he had been prepared to spend any money. His meanness was legendary: on his last appearance, as he was bowing his farewell and retreating up the stage, he said in a whisper to those in the wings, "Am I near; am I near?" "Very", said Liston, who was close by; "no one more so!"[18] When he died, many of the parts he had laboured to make famous died with him. He was a comedian of the old school, a man of the late eighteenth century: it was left to Liston to embody in his career, more than any other comedian, the development from the comedy of the eighteenth century to the farce, sometimes broad, sometimes domestic, that characterised the middle years of the nineteenth century.

During the summer of 1824 Liston returned again to the Haymarket Theatre. *Sweethearts and Wives* was revived and proved as popular as ever. One evening, when he entered as Billy Lackaday, he was actually applauded by the audience, a custom not then so prevalent in the theatre. Another revival was *Killing No Murder* and one night, during Apollo Belvi's dancing scene, Liston slipped and ripped his trousers. The audience was so amused, it insisted on an encore: Liston obliged them, returning to the stage with a large handkerchief dangling over the aperture. Despite his success in these old favourites, he also undertook a number of new roles, the most outstanding of which was Van Dunder, a foolish Dutch burgomaster in John Poole's *'Twould Puzzle a Conjuror*. This *Pl. 21* had been adapted from an earlier play of Poole's, *The Burgomaster of Sardaam*, (which had been condemned at Covent Garden in 1818), and turned into a vehicle for Liston. The play was still considered weak, but Liston's character, whose perplexed catch-phrase gives the play its title, won over the audience, especially when Liston, in baggy Dutch bloomers and ludicrously buckled shoes, came forward after the first performance to announce its repetition.

Liston did not return to Drury Lane after the Haymarket season, for on 23 July Drury Lane and Covent Garden had agreed to restore the one year gap between engagements at the two theatres and to reduce salaries to no more than £20 per week or £10 per night. The agreement further stipulated that there were to be no clear benefits or additional payments to any performers. Liston may have considered a Drury Lane engagement was of little value on such terms, though he had already announced in May that he would be touring the provinces during the forthcoming year. Both theatres also agreed not to employ Madame Vestris during the new season, but Kean was eventually re-engaged at Drury Lane, apparently at as high a salary as ever.

In the autumn Liston and his wife left their home in Soho Square – they would soon be moving to St. George's Place in Brompton – and set off for Birmingham. Liston now ran his own carriage and was one of the few contemporary actors affluent enough to do so. Considering the frequency of his tours he was lucky, perhaps, never to meet any mishap although he once slipped and hurt his hip whilst alighting.[19] From Birmingham he travelled onwards to catch the boat to Dublin, where he was engaged from 22 November. He was looking forward to this visit, for his old friend Abbott was now managing the Dublin Theatre and Charles Mathews was currently appearing there. Although Liston and Mathews attracted crowded houses, they were not happy with their reception. Liston grumbled at the £230 he received for his benefit, even though Mathews received only £170 for his.[20] In 1828 Mathews sent a letter to Alfred Bunn, who had taken over the management of the Dublin Theatre, saying that he and Liston had sworn a joint-oath never to appear in Dublin again:

I never liked Ireland – wrote Mathews. – Ireland never liked or understood me. I do not *hate* them for this, but I thoroughly hate them for their want of appreciation of Liston. We acted there together often – not the last engagement. They would not smile at him – they broke his heart; and he is a mean hound if he allows them to annoy him again. . . . Therefore do not lament me or Liston, who would have got less than me, had he not secured £10 per night certain.[21]

Liston kept his vow never to appear in Dublin again. When, in 1832, he was invited to pay a farewell visit to Ireland, he refused, saying:

No – they have seen me for the last time; they don't laugh at my jokes they hiss all my new pieces, and I am rich enough not to expose myself to unnecessary mortification.[22]

Liston was more fortunate in the towns and cities of England and Scotland, where a visit from the comedian had become almost an annual event. During the first three months of the new year he appeared at Exeter, Brighton, Bristol, Bath, Portsmouth, Southampton, Winchester and then undertook the arduous journey to Scotland, where he appeared at the Glasgow and Edinburgh theatres. Liston was a popular visitor to provincial theatres: he always entered the green-room with a cheery smile and looked around to see if there was any actor there whom he had met before. He had a remarkable memory for names and, on recognising an old acquaintance, he would grasp his hand cordially and express his pleasure at remeeting him. Walter Donaldson, a young actor in the Bristol company, remembered Liston's visits affectionately. Liston was so pleased with the young Donaldson's performance as the steward in *Fish Out of Water*, that he always requested the management to set him down for the part. He also promised to recommend Donaldson for an engagement at the Haymarket Theatre and kept his word, for, said Donaldson, he was a gentleman by birth and education.[23]

Another actor who found Liston very agreeable on his provincial tours was an ex-soldier, Benson Earl Hill, who met him in Cheltenham. Hill entertained Liston to dinner and introduced him to his eccentric landlord, a man by the name of Tully. Liston enjoyed meeting strangers, especially if they were in any way diverting, and soon put the company at ease. When Tully arrived, he enquired after the health of Liston and his wife, concluding every remark he made with, "Well, I'm very glad to hear it". This convulsed the company, as did Liston's look of sentimental admiration as he murmured:

"How gracious! glad of everything, bless him!"

Liston played gently on this peculiarity at the dinner-party, but seemed to have forgotten it by the next day. However, on the night when Hill played Young Marlow to Liston's Tony Lumpkin, Liston convulsed both Hill and the audience, by replying to Hill's every exclaimation:

"Well, I'm very glad to hear it".[24]

Back in London for the summer season, Liston soon found that he had not been out of the public eye, despite his prolonged absence. Ever since he had moved to Drury Lane, he had become the subject of a large number of critical articles and memoirs. In October, 1823, *The London Magazine* claimed that it looked on Liston's face "in the light of a national misfortune". Even though Liston was not a grimacier – "this actor does involuntarily what Munden does laboriously" – he had debased public taste and encouraged playwrights to mould parts to fit him. This was not altogether Liston's fault and, indeed, the commentator concluded his article by confessing that he could never suppress his amusement when he watched Liston perform.[25] A subsequent memoir in *The Drama*, in January 1824, felt that the problem lay more with the lack of parts equal to Liston's talents. This journal also commented on his uniqueness and originality. A further strength, noted by *The Mirror of the Stage* two months later, was the effortlessness of his performances and the seemingly undeliberate way in which he drew forth the audience's laughter.

While he was touring in the West Country early in 1825 Liston was amazed to read an extraordinary essay in *The London Magazine*,[26] purporting to be a biography of him. Written in deliberate parody of Johnson's *Lives of the Poets*, the piece contained much spurious information, which was willingly swallowed by a large cross-section of a gullible public and press. Liston's solemnity was attributed to a series of childhood bereavements and his development as a comic actor to an inability to control the comical faces that kept peeping out whenever he played tragedy. The anonymous author was Charles Lamb, who was delighted with the success of his hoax. A more improbable life for Liston to have lived could not easily have been invented. Crabb Robinson, who read it out to Lamb on a visit to his friend, privately felt it had little wit in it and that, if Liston were offended by it, Lamb would find it difficult to defend himself. Lamb, however, took the hoax further, publishing a very favourable review of the Liston Memoir in a subsequent edition of *The London Magazine*. He followed this up with a hoax letter from Munden, casting doubt on the truth of the Memoir and insisting that he would certainly not let the same thing happen to him.[27]

About the same time a somewhat more malevolent memoir of Liston appeared in a series known as *Oxberry's Dramatic Biography*. This memoir was compiled by the widow of William Oxberry, whose career as a comic actor had been somewhat eclipsed by Liston's popularity in the same line of roles. Oxberry had joined the Covent Garden company as a low comedian in 1807. Like Liston he was extremely ugly, a fact which led to frequent bantering between the two comedians as to who was the uglier. They even put the matter to the test on one occasion by attempting to frighten a horse away by staring at it, a contest which Liston won. Oxberry did not stay long at Covent Garden: the management had engaged him because Emery had threatened to leave. When Emery decided not to go, Oxberry found he had very little to do, so he eventually transferred to Drury Lane. In his spare time he ran a tavern: he was notoriously dissolute and became one of Kean's closest companions. He died in 1824 of an apoplectic fit brought on by heavy drinking. Although he never reached the front rank of comic performers, his wife believed that, with more time and study, he might have achieved a higher position in the profession than that achieved by Liston.

Just about every unfavourable detail that could be assembled against Liston appeared in Mrs. Oxberry's account. Liston was accused of severing his family ties, once he became famous; of aloofness from his fellow actors; and of heavy drinking. Few men, said Mrs. Oxberry, could down more wine at a sitting than Liston. Once, when he appeared at a benefit at the Croydon Theatre, he was so drunk that he could not stand up straight. He even, continued Mrs Oxberry, handled an elderly actress named Mrs. Collier so roughly that he tore half her dress off, forcing her to retire speedily from the stage. His indecency and buffoonery on stage were also criticised: one instance cited was his habit of wiping off the colouring from Wowski's face when he played Trudge in *Inkle and Yarico* and wiping it on his own. The managers, claimed Mrs Oxberry, directed their authors to write no comic parts for other actors that would mitigate against Liston leading the van. Even worse, actors on stage pretend to laugh at his jokes, even though they aren't very funny. "We consider him", she continued, "only a second rate comedian, yet we feel we then compliment him. Among his brother actors, *who know the tricks of the trade*, he is regarded as a successful quack: but we believe none, save and except newspaper critics, even considered him a *sterling* actor". He was, she concluded, a caricaturist rather than an actor, for when called upon to convey the heart and mind of a man, he was lost.[28]

Liston need not have worried about the venom with which the far from disinterested Mrs. Oxberry attacked him in this memoir. Even if there was a grounding of truth in some of the criticisms, the favour extended to him by his audiences belied many of the claims made against him. His broad, low characters, with their exaggerated and sometimes unpleasant characteristics, provided a comic portrait gallery of low life. When he first moved to Drury Lane, he was praised for his chaste and discriminating style of acting.[29] Indeed, when he resumed his annual engagement at the Haymarket Theatre early in 1825 he was to play a role which not only transcended all criticism, but was also to ensure him of his place as the outstanding comic actor of his generation.

Chapter VI

Paul Pry – 1825–1826

"Just dropped in. I hope I don't intrude".

When Liston first uttered this catch-phrase, at the Haymarket Theatre on 13 September, 1825, he had little idea of the furore he was about to create. He was playing the name-part in John Poole's new play, *Paul Pry*, about an interfering busybody unable to mind his own business. The play proved so popular that, before long, it was almost impossible to gain admission to the Haymarket on *Paul Pry* nights. Effigies of Liston as Paul Pry appeared everywhere: in the print shops, in the pottery warehouses, in the centre of pocket handkerchiefs, stamped on butter, adorning spill boxes, even in toyshops. Soon it was impossible to go into a front parlour without finding a figurine or toby jug of Liston as Paul Pry staring up at you from the mantelpiece. If you took a friendly pinch of snuff, you were likely to find Liston's features regarding you from the lid of the proffered box. Every pastry and print shop, troops of periodical papers, songs, sonnets, labels and letters, commented *The Age* (23/4/1826), were emblazoned with likenesses of Liston and conspired to whet public curiosity in a totally unprecedented way.

Paul Pry became one of the greatest theatrical hits of the age: it had one of the longest runs recorded since *The Beggar's Opera* and, at the height of its appeal, box prices were reputedly paid for gallery seats.[1] The author, John Poole, was thought to have based the character on a certain Tommy Hill. Hill was so inquisitive, he actually dined out on his knowledge of everybody's business. Not only could he regale his companions with all the latest scandal, he knew every detail of the domestic economy of his friends and would relate his knowledge to all and sundry. Poole disclaimed that Hill was his inspiration for Paul Pry, but nobody believed him.[2] The character, he said, had been suggested to him by an anecdote he heard about an inquisitive old lady. She could distinguish the sound of every door-knocker in the street, as she lay in her bed, and used to wonder what was going on in each house. In fact, he said, a number of people had been unconscious sources for the character, but it was not based upon one particular person. Poole felt it was a mark of the general truth with which he had created the character that Paul Pry was often thought to be based on somebody specific.[3] In fact, Paul Pry probably owed a little to Marplot in Mrs. Centilivre's *The Busybody*, whilst Poole freely acknowledged his use of a French play, *Le Vieux Celibataire*, as his source for the sub-plot.

Liston was at first dissatisfied with the part of Paul Pry and thought he could make little of this ignorant, but knowing, country busybody, who always knows everybody's business and always turns up when he is not wanted. He was disgusted by the fact that Paul Pry had little to do with the main plot and, when he turned up for the first rehearsal, he hadn't even bothered to learn his lines properly. Then, by chance, his attention was caught by a stage carpenter standing nearby, an odd figure with large cossack trousers tucked into high boots. This provided him with a hint as to costume and he began to take an interest in the character. In striped trousers, hessian boots, tail coat and top hat, he turned Paul Pry into an original creation. The costume, which became inseparable from the character, was soon enhanced by further details, such as a habit of taking snuff and a tendency to stare at everything through lorgnettes. Most memorable of all was the umbrella, which he conveniently left behind everywhere he visited, so that he would have an excuse to return and *Pls. 2(a),* eavesdrop a little further. These features stamped the character indelibly *25, 28(b)* on the public imagination, as did his catch-phrases, "I hope I don't intrude", "Just dropped in" and "Between ourselves". His habit of unexpectedly "dropping in" constantly brought the play alive, especially whenever it seemed to be flagging.

The main plot of *Paul Pry* concerns the problems caused by an arranged marriage between the daughter of Colonel Hardy, Eliza, and Harry Stanley, the son of one of Hardy's old friends. Harry and Eliza have met previously, unknown to their parents, and fallen in love, but they have no idea that the marriages planned for them will actually unite them. Many of the plot's complications arise from this fact and from Harry's presence, in disguise, in the neighbourhood, especially since Paul Pry chooses to interfere in their affairs. The sub-plot concerns the plans of a scheming housekeeper, Mrs. Subtle, to insinuate herself into the favours of her master, old Witherton, so that he will marry her and bequeath her his fortune. Some incriminating letters, which she throws down a well, are fished out by Paul Pry, whose curiosity exposes her duplicity and brings about a happy ending. The main plot is also resolved to everyone's satisfaction and Paul Pry concludes the play by boasting, in self-justification, that:

"A spirit of enquiry is the greatest characteristic of the age we live in."

In many ways *Paul Pry* was a rather old-fashioned comedy, brought to life largely by Liston's outstanding performance. John Genest, who did not think much of the play, praised Liston for "a perfect piece of acting" and for his "ease and good humour".[4] The *Times* (14/9/25) was happy to see Liston in a part at last worthy of his talents, whilst the *London Magazine* (November, 1825) liked the way in which he filled out the part "with a thousand nameless absurdities". Liston acted the character in a lively, humorous manner, but with a technique founded upon control and relaxation. Possibly the secret of his success as Paul Pry was his repose. Whether he appeared unexpectedly at a bedroom window, made himself at home where he was patently not wanted, laughed at presumed mis-spellings in letters that were none of his business, bent down at keyholes or dressed in the most outrageous angling outfit imaginable, he never failed to amuse. As Pry appeared in a sequence of almost farcical situations, he came very much to life in Liston's sharply observed portrayal.

One member of the audience recalled how everyone was particularly convulsed with laughter when Liston turned his back and stooped down to look through a keyhole, complaining all the time that keyholes were not properly made so as to suit the exigencies of an enquiring mind. His large, protuberant behind, so clearly depicted in prints of Paul Pry, excited much mirth whenever he bent over. This part of his anatomy was once the subject of an anecdote related of him. He got on a somewhat crowded omnibus where an old lady remarked, "Lor, sir, you've got nothing to sit upon". "Oh yes I have, ma'am", was the reply, "but I don't know where to put it!"[5]

Liston was praised for being:

> not only excellent in himself, but the cause of excellence in others; when he is on the stage, every other performer seems animated with a desire to contribute to the general good effect.[6]

Among the cast were William Farren and Madame Vestris, both of whom had helped to make *Sweethearts and Wives* such a success. Farren was perfectly cast as the huff-bluff Colonel Hardy and Madame Vestris contributed an arch, lively performance as Phoebe the maid. In the course of the play she introduced the song *Cherry Ripe*, which further enhanced its popularity. Mrs. Glover, as the treacherous housekeeper Mrs. Subtle, was highly praised for her convincing portrayal and the veteran actor Pope turned in a good performance as the old bachelor, Witherton.

Pope was something of a gourmet and Liston used to tease him about his refined taste in foods. When Liston spoke of a preference for boiled sucking-pig and haunches of venison, Pope would rush out of the green-room disgusted at Liston's depraved taste. One day Liston greeted Pope, saying:

"What do you think? My wine merchant has been endeavouring to impose on me by charging 80s a dozen for old Port, when I can get *new* with half the money, but I am not quite such a fool to be done in that way. And then, that French Brandy. I will never buy any of it, while I can get British".

"Why, then", asked Pope, "I suppose you would like turpentine?"

"I have no doubt", replied Liston, "that it would be very nice with water".

Pope found this all too much. As a result, when he later overheard a gentleman in the Haymarket Theatre, describing to Liston the various modes of cooking abroad, he said:

"Sir, I have not the honour of knowing you, but hearing your descant on cooking to my worthy friend Liston, whom I respect in private and admire in public, I must inform you, you are speaking to a man who has no more taste in the table than a Catalaw Indian".[7]

Although *Paul Pry* was the hit of the 1825 season, it entered the Haymarket repertoire at a late stage in the proceedings. The Haymarket had been open since April, with William Dowton as principal comedian for the first two months. When Liston returned in June, somewhat fatter after his provincial excursions, business immediately picked up and Liston played the title role in a successful musical revival of Kane O'Hara's burletta *Midas*. Apart from Paul Pry, two other new parts proved extremely memorable. As Grojan, in Caroline Boaden's *Quite Correct*, a dramatisation of Theodore Hook's novel *Doubts and Fears*, Liston's ludicrous anxiety to be *correct* caused much amusement. An innkeeper who takes everything literally, Grojan is greatly alarmed when one of his female guests proposes to "unbosom" herself to him and is forever suspicious of the moral turpitude of his guests. In *Roses and Thorns*, a new play by Joseph Lunn, Liston played Sir Hilary Heartease and provided a chastened portrayal of hearty good-nature.   *Pl. 28(a)*

Quite Correct was regularly paired with *Paul Pry*, which dominated the final two months of the season. *Paul Pry* was scheduled almost every night, although it was held in abeyance for a fortnight whilst Liston fulfilled a prior engagement at Birmingham. People were nightly flocking to the theatre and being turned away, for the house was usually filled within minutes after the doors were opened. The nightly receipts, normally £150 or less, were now around £270.[8] Liston was earning £60 weekly and it was reported that *Paul Pry* had earned about £12,000 for the Haymarket management.[9] In time Liston added extra touches to his performance. One of these was to offer Colonel Hardy his visiting card, after the Colonel had angrily knocked Paul's hat off his head, Another was to come in front of the curtain to announce repetition of the play the following night. After apologising for intruding, he would deposit his gamp-like umbrella in a corner of the stage, then announce that, if he did not intrude, he would appear again next night. He then bowed and retired, but appeared again a few minutes later, with his usual apology, stating he had forgotten his umbrella.[10] By the last night of the season it seemed astonishing that *Paul Pry* could not go on for ever:

> Will Liston ever finish? – Will Paul Pry ever disappear? – Will he be eternally thrusting himself forward to the infinite diversion of an inexhaustible public.[11]

Liston was clearly ill by this time, apparently suffering from lumbago. Several times during the last performance he had to be supported off the stage. When the play ended, he seemed reluctant to make a speech, until the other actors pushed him forward. He announced, in the character of Paul Pry, that he would be back next season, then bowed repeatedly and left the stage. He was soon back, however, to collect his umbrella, which, he said, he would otherwise have to leave there until next April.

Not long after the season had ended, Liston was walking along Bond Street, when his eye was caught by a figure in the window of the Derby Potteries' London Warehouse. He immediately walked in and purchased it, for it was a little figure of him as Paul Pry, charmingly modelled by *Cover* Samuel Keys.[12] He could have chosen other models as well, if he had wanted to. Staffordshire, Enoch Wood & Son and Rockingham had all produced figures of Liston as Paul Pry; Wood and Rockingham had produced toby jugs as well. Some years later, when he came to illustrate *Oliver Twist*, George Cruikshank included a little figure of Paul Pry on Mrs. Corney's mantelpiece in his illustration of Mr. Bumble and Mrs. Corney taking tea. Liston, in fact, became a very popular subject with the potteries: Sam Swipes, Van Dunder, Lubin Log, Mawworm, Moll Flaggon and Dominie Sampson were among other Liston parts reproduced ceramically during this period.

Inn signs, milk jugs, tea pots, even a stage coach known as the "Paddington Paul Pry" bore Liston's likeness. There were Paul Pry songbooks, and a dance known as the Paul Pry Quadrille. Magazines appeared, named after the character, and the print shops were full of carricatures of Liston. Some of these prints, which often provided the sources from which the porcelain figures were modelled, were straightforward likenesses of Liston in the part, but others were used for political or social satires, showing Paul Pry enquiring into the abuses of chancery, *Pl. 27* electioneering, lotteries, banking and many other topics. One of the most amusing prints depicted Liston as Paul Pry gazing at Venus, scantily clad in linen drapery. The caption beneath was:

> They've got me in the print shops; they have upon my honour –
> I'm next to Venus, which they say, is quite a libel on her.[13]

A more sinister print showed Paul Pry sitting in a bed, confronted by Death in the form of a skeleton with a scythe. "Really, sir", says Pry, I'm almost sure I *never* saw your face before!" "Hope I don't intrude!" replies Death.

The fame attendant on Liston's popularity as Paul Pry did have its drawbacks, even if it won him the accolade of appearing as a waxwork at Madame Tussaud's.[14] Once, as he walking along Piccadilly with Charles Kemble, he was startled when a man whom he had never seen before called out from the top of a passing stage coach, "How are you, Paul Pry?". When Liston was travelling by coach to Brighton, a gentleman climbed in saying "I hope I don't intrude" and, when he discovered the coach was full, climbed out again, still quoting lines from the play. One sunday one of the newspapers reported a rather more alarming story, which may have been apocryphal. A melancholy gentleman, fond of frequenting the Haymarket, was so disappointed with seeing *Paul Pry* continually in the bills that, in a moment of despair, he made an attempt to assassinate Liston as he was getting into his carriage. The weapon only grazed Liston's cheek, but entered the body of a footman who was holding open the door of the carriage. The assassin, claimed the newspaper, was instantly secured.[15]

Over forty years later *The Times* (31/8/1866) recalled the furore that *Paul Pry* had created:

> Liston's figure ... was sure to be seen everywhere – on the walls of the Royal Academy, in the penny sheet of the theatrical print-seller, and on the image-board of the itinerant Italian. Fairs were then in vogue, and Paul Pry became one of the stock figures in the larger booths, likewise ornamenting the the signs of gingerbread stalls, and the carts belonging to the vendors of ginger-pop. Go where you would 40 years ago, you could not, by any means, avoid Paul Pry; the stern Puritan, by some

means or other, knew his face as well as the most inveterate playgoer . . . and his constantly recurring phrase "I hope I don't intrude" became a constant element in the "chaff" of the London street-boy.

In one of the many addresses written for Liston to perform as Paul Pry, reference is made to the multitude of forms into which his figure had been adapted:

> They shew me off in every form and way;
> In paper, pewter, plaster, brass and clay;
> In tea pot, milk pot, *other* pot and jug,
> They even make me out *an ugly mug.*
> When Christmas comes, I dare say for my sake,
> They'll set me dancing on an iced twelfth cake;
> And little boys and girls, no doubt, will eat me
> Like canibals – This is the way they treat me.[16]

Not only did Liston deliver addresses such as this; there were songs as well, including the popular "Adventures of Paul Pry". Once a letter was published in a journal, purportedly from Paul Pry, complaining that he had not been allowed to sing a song on stage on New Year's Eve, in the character of Mr. Liston.[17] Indeed, just about every ounce of fun possible was extracted from Paul Pry and every use possible made of him.

Although Liston's performance as Paul Pry was matchless, the character soon began to appear elsewhere. An actor made up to resemble Liston as Paul Pry was introduced by Farley into the Christmas Harlequinade at Covent Garden, *Harlequin and the Magic Rose.* Paul Pry was also introduced into J. R. Planché's Christmas burlesque, *Success* or *A Hit if You Like,* at the Adelphi Theatre. Douglas Jerrold turned the play into a farce for the Coburg Theatre in 1826; it was burlesqued at Astley's; in *Paul Pry on Horseback*, Pry actually jumped through the bar window of an inn on horseback. Another version, *Paul Pry Just Dropt In*, was specially written for Richardson's Travelling Theatre. In 1862 *Paul Pry* was americanised when J. S. Clarke played in his own adaptation of *Paul Pry in New York.*[18]

In time Paul Pry became the *sine qua non* of comic actors: the Lear or Hamlet of the low comedian. According to Percy Fitzgerald, writing in the 1870s:

> Every comic performer of any claims, as he advances to eminence, is called on to give his reading of "Paul Pry", and since Liston, who originally created the part fifty years ago, a vast number of facetious players have failed or succeeded in the attempt.[19]

John Reeve, J. B. Buckstone, David Rees, Edward Wright and J. L. Toole all essayed the part, whilst in America W. E. Burton, James K. Hackett and J. S. Clarke were among the actors to attempt Paul Pry. In 1834, in England, Mrs. Glover played Paul Pry for her benefit. The *Theatrical Observer* (9/10/34) regretted that a woman of such talent should have found it necessary to do something as outrageous and called it "a disgusting exhibition". Wright and Toole were the two most faithful of Liston's successors, preserving both the costume and manner with which Liston had originally invested the character. Toole, who first played the part in London in 1866, long remained popular in the role, although one critic felt he was so intense at times that he almost made Paul Pry into a semi-tragic figure.[20] But the actor upon whom Liston's performance was most influential was probably Henry Compton. When *Paul Pry* took the town by storm, Compton was still a boy, apprenticed to his uncle, a rather puritanical cloth merchant. Although they did not normally go to the theatre, the uncle stretched a point on this occasion, intrigued by the fashion for the new play. To the young Compton Liston's performance was a revelation. For days and weeks afterwards, with umbrella in hand, he would stride up and down his uncle's drawing room, in imitation of Liston's performance. He determined to go on the stage and, when he eventually achieved his ambition, Paul Pry became one of his regular parts.[21]

When the play re-opened at the Haymarket Theatre at the beginning of the 1826 season, the rage for it had in no way abated. Liston continued to delight audiences with his impersonation and returned again to the Haymarket in 1829, when *Paul Pry* proved as popular as ever. He could now command vast salaries and it was rumoured that he was receiving £50–£60 per night for his performance as Paul Pry.[22] His success was remarkable and confirmed even further his reputation as the outstanding comic actor of the day. After twenty years on the London stage, he had at last created his masterpiece. Although his popularity never waned, there was not to be another part quite so memorable as Paul Pry — he had, at last, reached the summit of his career.

Why *Paul Pry* should have been the subject of such adulation is difficult to say. The play was not particularly outstanding and Liston had created other characters who were just as distinctive. Whether it was public caprice, the genius of Liston or a combination of the two, *Paul Pry* became one of the most fashionable plays of its era and was still being revived in the 1890s.[23] There was no logical explanation for the Paul Pry craze: it just happened, without any of the help provided for such phenomena today through the media and modern marketing techniques. Not until Sothern played Lord Dundreary later in the century was a character again to take such a hold upon the public.

Chapter VII

The Star – 1826–1828

The streets around Drury Lane were blocked: Russell Street was impassable on account of the number of carriages parked there, and Vinegaryard swarmed with playgoers. An uninformed observer might have been forgiven, four days before Christmas, for assuming that the turn out was for the new pantomime. In fact, these playgoers had not come to watch the pantomime, but to welcome back their old favourite, Liston, whose success as Paul Pry had turned him into the most fashionable actor of the moment. He was greeted with three rounds of applause on his first appearance, by one of the largest and most elegant audiences assembled in the theatre for ages, and was cheered throughout the evening. This enthusiastic response was echoed throughout his short engagement at the theatre.[1]

Liston had soon recovered from the illness that assailed him on the last night of the Haymarket season, for within a week he had departed for Plymouth. He had made no immediate plans to engage at either of the patent theatres, although Covent Garden had tried to lure him earlier in the year. Liston, who had a strong sense of his own value as well as a sharp business acumen, had been incensed by the letter he had received from Covent Garden, offering him employment at either £10 per night or £20 per week. He took the letter straight back to Forbes, the Covent Garden treasurer, and asked if he were authorised to make such an offer – to him, a man of property, capable of earning £200 per week and able to support any theatre with only three parts.[2]

Drury Lane had been slow to make a move, despite the fashion for Liston created by *Paul Pry*. Elliston was recovering from the after-effects of a stroke and trying to cope with the manoeuverings of the Drury Lane Committee who were anxious to oust him. The compact with Covent Garden had proved a disastrous step: as no stars were engaged, attendances were poor and the theatre was losing money. In November, when the Committee had taken over the management of the theatre, they approached Liston and offered him a large sum to appear for a short engagement. James Winston, the acting manager, was very annoyed with the dramatist, Kenney, during these negotiations. Kenney, who had been appointed part of the management by Elliston, encouraged Liston to ask for a much larger sum than initially agreed to and, within two days of the first negotiations, Liston was back at the theatre, declining to sign his contract. The Committee was so eager to have him back, they agreed to anything and made it a personal favour that he should sign. His engagement infuriated not only Winston, who felt that high salaries were injuring Drury Lane financially, but also Charles Kemble. He wrote to Drury Lane, reminding them of the compact between the two theatres; before long another letter was despatched, warning Drury Lane that *Love, Law and Physic* was Covent Garden's property and not to be performed elsewhere.[3]

Liston was soon comfortably installed in Drury Lane, with his usual dresser, Bankes, to attend to him. He was worried, though, about his wife, who had been ill, but by early January she had begun to recover. Ann Mathews sometimes dropped by to sit with her during the day and regale her with the latest letter from young Charles, now twenty two, who was then up in Scotland.[4] By the end of the month Liston felt able to leave her again and set off on another excursion into the country.

Liston spent the next two months touring the provinces, all eagerly awaiting a taste of *Paul Pry*. He visited Bath and Bristol, spent a couple of nights appearing in Brighton, then continued to Portsmouth and to the Hampshire theatres he had visited the previous year. Great excitement was caused in Taunton, when it was announced that Liston would make his first appearance there for 26 years. He performed on three alternate nights during the second week of March to the delight of Taunton's inhabitants and its neighbourhood. While in Taunton he sought out the surviving people that he knew, including his former landlady, and impressed himself as "a gentleman of courteous and unobtrusive manners, of cultivated taste and benevolent disposition".[5] He then departed for Cheltenham, where he was to stay a fortnight for the improvement of his health.

The summer season at the Haymarket, which Liston rejoined in April, was still dominated by *Paul Pry*. No other new part could compete, although Poole created a new Liston role, the Cornish hypochondriac Simon Pengander, in a farce *Twixt the Cup and the Lip*, first performed on *Pl. 24* 12 June. Indeed, only one new attraction captured popular attention that year. For Liston's Haymarket benefit, on Monday 18 September, Madame Vestris appeared in a new character, as a Dutch girl, and sang Alexander Lee's arrangement of *Buy a Broom* to the old German air of *Leil* or *Augustine*. The ballad proved so popular that, with *Paul Pry*, it formed a regular part of the bill until the end of the season. When Madame Vestris's benefit took place on 6 November, Liston dressed as a broom girl

Pl. 26   and they sang the ballad as a duet. The combination of the dainty, diminutive Vestris with the grotesque and ludicrous comedian proved irresistable, especially when Liston sang the second verse:

> For Brushes and Beauty there's none can excel us,
> Little sister is budding and I'm in the bloom;
> So, Ladies, I pray, of my face don't be jealous,
> What youth can refuse when I cry "Buy a Broom".

Accompanying it with an absurd parody of the waltz, Liston often
Pl. 23   repeated the ballad at subsequent benefits.[6]

During the Haymarket season Liston was occasionally absent, to fulfil provincial engagements. In June he had performed again in Brighton and in October he visited Birmingham and Chester. His popularity was still immense: at Birmingham the theatre was so overcrowded that Liston was re-engaged for an extra appearance. Indeed, Liston's attraction was so great when starring in the provinces, that he received from £250 to £350 as his share of the receipts for one week in such towns as Manchester, Birmingham and Liverpool.[7] Provincial theatres often suspended their free list when Liston was engaged and sometimes even raised the price of admission.

After the Haymarket engagement was over, Liston and his wife spent a month or two residing in Brighton. Liston was not only a popular performer at the Brighton Theatre, but also very much a part of the fashionable set that congregated there. Remarkable for the suavity of his manners and the ease of his deportment, he encountered no difficulty in mixing in high society. His adherence to the fashionable life was further reflected in the Picadilly address to which he moved in London, although it was not long before he moved back to St. George's Place again. On 1 December, 1826, he had to leave his wife in Brighton and travel up to London, for the King had asked to see Liston as Lubin Log at a Command performance at Drury Lane. On the occasion of this perform-ance Liston had the task of lighting the King to his Box, in return for which the King honoured him by shaking his hand. Liston then remained in London for another ten days before rejoining Sarah in Brighton, after regretfully declining a dinner invitation from the comedian Knight for the following Sunday.[8]

Late in 1826 Liston signed a contract to appear at Drury Lane, now under the management of the American Stephen Price, for the remainder of the season. Liston was now irrefutably a "star", a term which received much discussion in the press of the time. The "star" system was blamed, wrongly in many ways, for the financial hardship under which the patent theatres were struggling. In all discussions of the star system Liston was usually cited as a principal culprit amid the galaxy of names which could attract large salaries. Economically, though, the "star" system was viable: when the Covent Garden defaulters joined Drury Lane in 1823, at vastly increased salaries, the annual takings for the theatre rose by £10,000.[9] Price certainly showed no sign of abolishing it: like his predecessors, he relied on old favourites such as Liston, who could draw large audiences single-handed.

As a star, of course, Liston had the right to veto the parts he played. For the new season the playwright George Soane was offered £150 for a comedy and two melodramas, provided Liston agreed to play in the comedy. After reading Soane's *The Trial of Love*, Liston sent a written undertaking to Price that he would play Antonio in the new play, although it did not prove too successful in performance.[10] Thomas Dibdin the playwright recounts how, some years earlier, he had taken a new play to Liston for his approval, before Morris would accept it at the Haymarket. Dibdin read the play to Liston over breakfast at Liston's home, during which Liston told Dibdin that he regretted the practice of always asking him to sit in judgement on authors.[11] Even so, after the years of drudgery at Covent Garden, Liston was probably relieved that he now had the power to select only the parts he wished to play.

Liston's most successful role during the new season was Sir Hippington Miff in R. B. Peake's *Comfortable Lodgings*, first performed on 10 March. Sir Hippington is an English travelling gentleman, who is informed by the Minister of Police in France that he is to be robbed and perhaps murdered in the "comfortable lodgings" where he is staying, but that he must not betray his fears. Crabb Robinson found Liston's "humorous fears and anxieties" "exquisitely comic"[12], a view endorsed by the German Prince Puckler Muskau, then on a visit to England. He was particularly amused by a scene in which Liston suspected the hostess of the inn of trying to poison him with a cup of chocolate:

> In a transport of rage and terror Liston seizes her by the throat and forces her to drink the chocolate: which, after some surprise at the oddness of English manners, she very willingly does. Liston's by-play during this, and the manner in which, suddenly recollecting his promise, he bursts into a convulsive laugh, and tries to turn it off as a jest, is unspeakably droll.[13]

Another highlight of the play was Liston's gloomy, melancholy description of how a temptation to lapse from virtue under the amorous provocations of a dry-salter's wife had forced him to travel abroad. His ability to be deadpan on stage was deliberately played upon when his servant asked him why he couldn't laugh, as other people do. "Laugh!" he exclaimed, in a tone from the bottom of his chest and with the bitter emphasis of a misanthrope — "laugh! I cannot do as other people do! When I look round me" (here he looked at the pit with a dull stare) "I see everyone laughing and merry. While my face remains immoveable as the face carved on a brass knocker!" Even worse, he couldn't be seasick like all the other passengers on the packet-boat. "I look on", he said, "*a disappointed man!*"[14]

The life of a "star" was exhausting and, by the summer, Liston had decided to take a well-earned rest. He spent a part of the summer in Kent, but he was summoned back into activity in September by a request from his old friend, William Abbott. Abbott had recently been offered and accepted the post of manager at the Théâtre Favart in Paris, where he planned to hold a season of English drama. The company was to be led by Charles Kemble, Macready and, in comedy, by Liston. Liston, in fact, opened the season as Bob Acres in *The Rivals* on 5 September. The original opening date had been deferred, because a deputation of French actors had complained to the Minister of Justice about the English venture. Even when this problem had been resolved, further problems arose on the second night of the company's performing. Liston was to have played Lubin Log in *Love, Law and Physic*, but the play was not permitted as it had not been submitted to the French dramatic censorship. So *She Stoops to Conquer* was hastily substituted, with Liston as Tony Lumpkin. Harriet Smithson, soon to captivate the French composer Hector Berlioz, played Miss Hardcastle.

Acres was not one of Liston's best parts, though his cowardice in the duel scene was often praised. The French, accustomed to the lighter boulevard humour of Baptiste cadet and to the intellectual comedy of Potier, were disappointed in Liston, whom they thought had been over-rated. One journal referred to "la triste mediocrité"[15] of Liston and, although Tony Lumpkin restored the balance slightly, Liston drew little laughter. The French, said Hazlitt, would:

> have no more notion how we should have such an actor as Liston on our stage than if we were to tell them we have parts performed by a sea-otter; nor if they were to see him, would they be much the wiser, or know what to think of his unaccountable twitches of countenance or non-descript gestures, of his teeth chattering in his head, his eyes that seem dropping from their sockets, his nose that is tickled by a jest as by a feather and shining with self-complacency as if oiled, his ignorant

conceit, his gazing stupor, his lumpish vivacity in Lubin Log or Tony Lumpkin.[16]

The English, claimed Hazlitt, had a less sophisticated sense of humour than the French — they abandoned themselves to mirth without having to find a reason for their laughter. For Liston the matter was more simple: he considered the lukewarm response of the French was a slight and refused Abbott's offer of another engagement, denouncing the French in the Drury Lane green-room as a set of jack-asses.[17]

In the meantime, Stephen Price was very eager to have Liston back for the new season at Drury Lane. He had set his hopes on a joint-engagement of Liston and Mathews, renewing their partnership in some of the roles they had been playing twenty years before at the Haymarket Theatre. Price told Mathews that he could name his own terms and asked him to help him persuade Liston to join them for the season. Mathews had not performed at a patent theatre for over a decade: he had left Covent Garden, dissatisfied with the mediocre parts he was offered to play. He had a hankering to play the classical comedy roles — parts like Falstaff or Sir Anthony Absolute — and felt under-used. His lameness also made acting difficult and he concentrated increasingly on his one-man shows. The return of Mathews to one of the patent theatres was therefore likely to be something of an event.

The friendship between Mathews and Liston had continued. They frequently dined together and once, when Liston failed to secure the purchase of a house near to Mathews' in Highgate, he actually shed tears like a child.[18] The two comedians frequently played practical jokes on one another. One morning Mathews called on Liston, who was making a late toilette. After waiting a few minutes, he told Sarah Liston he was in haste and asked leave to go to her husband's dressing room. He knocked and, in a child's voice, requested that the door might be opened, as he had "a message from Mr. Mathews" to deliver. Liston believing his own boy was at the door, told him to go downstairs, as he would follow as soon as possible. When the voice persisted in its request, Liston was so exasperated that he flung open the door, only to discover Charles Mathews standing there.[19] At times Mathews and his wife could be rather querulous. Whenever Mathews toured the provinces, a vast number of letters passed between them, usually full of recriminations against each other for not writing regularly enough. Ann Mathews was especially touchy and Sarah Liston fell foul of her more than once. Only recently, when Mathews had been exhibiting his latest "At Home" to a party of friends, she had reprimanded her for not laughing and applauding her husband's efforts enough.[20]

Liston was soon enticed back to Drury Lane, reappearing in many old favourites. Kenney also provided him with a new cockney part, in many ways a worthy successor to Lubin Log and Billy Lackaday. This was *Pl. 29* Bowbell, a London merchant, in *The Illustrious Stranger*, first staged on 4 October. When Liston entered, despairingly casting his eyes up to heaven and wearing a soaking-wet, tattered costume, with a hat which had almost lost its crown, the audience roared, especially when Liston told them he was now fit for roasting, being covered in dripping. Shipwrecked on a desert island, the forlorn and cowardly Bowbell laments his fate until he is mistaken by the native islanders for an illustrious stranger and married off to their Princess, an honour he accepts with typical cockney complacency. Unfortunately, his reign is short-lived, for the Princess is reported dead and Bowbell learns that custom dictates he is to be buried alive with her. When Liston entered in his own funeral procession, in a long white gown and ridiculous bonnet, he turned to the audience with such a look of pathetic despair that they couldn't help laughing. His ludicrous joy, once a substitute victim was found, added another touch of humour to Liston's portrayal of this bumptious cockney.

During December Liston travelled northwards, to appear in Manchester and Liverpool. It was at Liverpool, on 12 December, that he met with an unfortunate accident. Whilst playing Billy Lackaday he was required to sink back into a chair, overcome by the touch of the beautiful Laura: he misjudged the distance on this particular evening and struck his hip a severe blow on the chair as he fell. He consequently had to cancel his engagement at Manchester and spend a week in Liverpool recuperating, before completing his engagement there a couple of weeks before Christmas.[21] Even in the new year, when he was performing on alternate nights at Drury Lane, he was not deterred from making further provincial engagements. Although he declined an engagement at the Norwich Theatre, he was prepared to journey down to Brighton during February to play on alternate nights and, in March, travelled down to Bath to perform for several nights.[22]

The renewal of Liston's partnership with Mathews was to take place on New Year's Eve. Mathews had been employed at an extremly high salary, so high, in fact, that he had felt guilty at first about accepting it. The night prior to his appearance he was depressed: he was sure the venture would prove a failure and not attract audiences. He was unconvinced that such tired old pieces as *The Critic* and *Killing No Murder* could still retain their appeal. He need not have worried: there was so great a crowd assembled, it was almost impossible to get into the theatre. The two comic actors still fitted together like parts in a jigsaw puzzle, "each prominent where the other retires".[23] The house was crammed on successive nights; the pit was overflowing; and the receipts were greater than those that Kean had commanded during the previous season.[24]

Mathews was amazed that the theatre could be filled out with such "hackneyed" pieces, but before long he and Liston appeared together in a new piece especially written for them. As the grasping Tom Tadpole in Peake's *The Haunted Inn* Liston had a far better part than the whimsical corporal assigned to Mathews. Ann Mathews was rather jealous of Liston's success in this play, claiming that the part of Tadpole had been written for her husband, but that he had magnanimously resigned it to Liston, for whom he felt it was more suited. She considered that he was being over-delicate and that he caused Price considerable embarrassment by declining the part.[25] Mathews, however, was right: the part of Tom Tadpole could have been played by none other than Liston and Mathews ably supported him in the role of Corporal Trot.

The Mathews-Liston partnership was largely dominated by revivals. *Love for Love* was given an airing, with Liston as Ben and Mathews as Foresight. A number of Colman's comedies were revived, including *The Gay Deceivers*, *The Poor Gentleman* and *Who Wants a Guinea*. In *A School for Scandal* Mathews essayed Sir Peter Teazle, whilst Liston renewed acquaintance with his old stock part of Sir Benjamin Backbite. These classic comedies, combined with more recent pieces, provided a bill that awakened the nostalgia of the old, whilst whetting the curiosity of the young. Price was so pleased with the success of the season, he desired to renew Mathews' engagement for the following year, but Mathews declined. The physical effort of acting on the large Drury Lane stage was making his lameness worse and he opted to return to the Adelphi, to continue with his less debilitating "At Homes".

Liston met Mathews again during the summer, while fulfilling a number of engagements on the south coast. From Southampton and Worthing he had continued to Brighton, where his arrival with his wife at the Old Ship Hotel was announced in the "Fashionable Chronicle" of the *Brighton Gazette* (17/7/28). Mathews was on tour in Brighton, performing an "At Home", which Liston went to see. Whilst Mathews was singing his auction song, in the course of which he solicited biddings for a particular lot, he looked round the house, exclaiming "only three pounds off, only three!" Suddenly, a voice from one of the public boxes cried out "Four". The voice was unmistakeable and, when the audience and Mathews looked towards its source, so was the countenance. Mathews joined in the joke, knocking the object down to Liston. Liston told Ann Mathews afterwards that he had been seized with an irresistable desire to make a bid and had been most surprised both at himself and at the roar of laughter and notice he attracted.[26]

Liston himself appeared at the Brighton Theatre on 29 July as Paul Pry before a very fashionable audience which included the Dukes of Cambridge, Devonshire and Richmond. He was the great popular favourite of the day. John Bannister, the veteran comic actor, whom Liston affectionately used to call his old "Papa", reckoned that Liston was still holding his ground against Kean and Vestris.[27] With the exception of Kean he was the only actor to draw single-handed. People were now going to the theatre, not to see a particular play, but to see Liston.[28] He was one of the great "stars" of the day, at the very top of his profession.

Chapter VIII

New Directions – 1828–1831

> A substantial farmer, blunt, honest and humane; a joker, a smoker and
> a laughing philosopher to boot.[1]

Such a description does not sound like a typical Liston role. Yet, as Adam
Brock, the genial, good-natured farmer in J. R. Planché's *Charles XII*, Liston scored one of his greatest successes. The play was first performed at Drury Lane on 11 December, 1828, and Liston was praised for his "delightful picture of the kind-hearted humourist"[2] and for his "very subdued yet excellent acting".[3] Ben Webster reckoned that Liston's performance dispelled, once and for all, the notion that he was a mere "face-maker".[4] The management at Drury Lane considered the part right out of his line – they would have preferred him as the officious clerk Muddlewerk, a part eventually assigned to Harley – but he had taken to it eagerly and played it with such success that his performance was nominated "the perfection of comic acting".[5] Liston used to tell Planché, with whom he soon became firm friends, that the playwright had given him the opportunity of making a new reputation.

The highlight of the play is a scene in which Charles XII visits Adam Brock incognito, in order to repay a voluntary war-loan sent to him many years ago by Brock. Brock openly speaks his mind about the King's laxness and is astonished when his visitor's true identity is accidentally revealed. William Farren played the King – he had recently reneged on his contract with Covent Garden and his defection to Drury Lane was to cost him heavy damages. For once he was playing a character of his own age, instead of the old men he usually specialised in. He was highly praised for his performance; like Liston, he was deemed to have added new honours to his name. Liston's performance was considered the perfection of art and nature united:

> for unless they were combined, the rough hearty old farmer could not be
> so perfect, no acting could give so truly the bluff joyous heartiness,

Pl. 30(a)

73

without some touch of the real feeling of kind-heartedness; Liston's
Adam Brock makes us think better of our species ...[6]

The *Athenaeum* was delighted that, for once, Liston had "thrown aside his
usual imitation of mirth-moving dullness and dogged ill-nature", replac-
ing it with so delightful a portrait of the merry and sagacious farmer.[7]

The success of this play encouraged Planché to write several more
historical dramas for Liston and Farren over the next three years. Liston's
role of Monsieur Papelard, a self-interested and vacillating politician in
Partizans (1829), led the *Court Journal* (23 May, 1829) to praise Planché,
who:

has undoubtedly been the person to call forth in this singular actor, not
merely a power which few (himself not among the exceptions) believed
him to possess, but a power which is worth all his others put together –
namely, that of representing actual nature, in a perfectly simple and
natural and therefore ... a perfectly effective and highly amusing
manner.

Achille Bonbon in *The National Guard* (1830) and Pierre in *The Legion of
Honour* (1831) proved more conventional: they failed to provide the same
sort of scope as Adam Brock. Nevertheless, *Charles XII* had started
something of a vogue for this sort of historical drama and before long other
dramatists followed Planché's lead, including James Kenney, who
fashioned for Liston the part of Joseph Addlewitz, a foolish miller, in *Peter
the Great*.

Liston remained friendly with Planché for the remainder of his life.
Through Liston Planché made the acquaintance of Sir David Wilkie the
artist, who had used Liston as a model for one of the characters in his
painting "The Ale-House Door". Although he felt Liston was an extremely
shy man, Planché also found him a source of great amusement. He recalled a children's party he held, which was attended by Liston dressed
like a small boy in a red coat, yellow cotton trousers and a dirty pinafore.
Thus attired, he insisted on sitting on the lap of Planché's old step-
mother, who was a great favourite with him. Planché and Liston
disagreed good-humouredly about burlesque. When Planché insisted on
elegant and accurate costuming for his extravaganzas at the Olympic
Theatre, Liston could not see the need for such reforms. "Liston thought
to the last", said Planché, "that Prometheus, instead of the Phrygian cap,
tunic and trousers, should have dressed like a great lubberly boy, in a red
jacket and nankeens, with a pinafore all besmeared with lollipops".[8]
Liston, of course, had played in a number of burlesques, including *Tom*

Thumb, The Critic, Bombastes Furioso and *Midas*, but it was a form in which he played infrequently at the time of which Planché was writing. Whatever their difference of opinion over this matter, they both, in their different ways, helped to bring about a more natural style of presentation in the early nineteenth century theatre.

When Liston rejoined the Haymarket company in the summer of 1829, he was again praised for those qualities which had been noted in Adam Brock. As Mr. Gillman in J. B. Buckstone's *The Happiest Day of My Life*, a farce which anticipated the growing interest in domestic situations within the genre, Liston was praised for his pleasing and natural mode of playing the part, without recourse to caricature or distortion. As a middle-aged man marrying a much younger wife, on whose long-anticipated wedding day everything goes wrong, a tearful Liston "marked the alternations of joy, vexation, jealousy and rage with great nicety and comical effect".[9] Mrs. Humby and Mrs. Glover, as the vulgar bride and her mother, helped with Liston to convey to the audience a convincing illusion of life as it really was. A few years later, as the hypocritical Janus in another domestic farce by Buckstone, *Snakes in the Grass*, Liston was again praised for his "admirably natural acting".[10]

Mr. Gillman, Adam Brock and Paul Pry were the mainstays of the Haymarket season, but for his benefit at the end of the season Liston decided to play a role completely outside his normal line of parts. He announced in the playbills that he would *attempt* Baron Wildenheim in *Lovers' Vows*. Wildenheim was a heavy father, a German nobleman of almost tragic dimensions, whom Liston had last played in his early days as a provincial actor. Liston seems to have conveyed the character adequately, despite exciting a certain degree of merriment among his audience, but usually his attempts at serious roles were doomed to failure. In May 1809, when the Covent Garden company was resident at the Haymarket, Liston had played Octavian for his benefit in George Colman's *The Mountaineers*. The audience were puzzled as to what to make of his performance of the love-lorn recluse: he acted the part seriously and sensibly, but the audience found him most ludicrous when he was most in earnest and laughter was soon the order of the evening. Three years later, for his wife's Covent Garden benefit, he played Romeo to the Juliet of Sarah Booth. However serious his intentions, he must have soon transmuted the part into burlesque.

Many rumours persisted that Liston had embarked on his professional career with a desire to play tragedy, a desire that he allegedly retained throughout his career. Ann Mathews, William Hazlitt and William Makepeace Thackeray were amongst those who referred to this desire, perpetuating a legend that might well be unfounded. For, if Liston ever

seriously thought he could become a tragic actor, he must have been
singularly unaware of his bizarre appearance. The very idea led G. H.
Lewes to comment:

> There has always been to me something pathetic in the thought of
> Liston, with his grave and serious turn of mind, his quick sensibilities,
> and his intense yearning for applause, fatally classed by Nature among
> those to whom tragic expression was impossible – feeling within him
> tragic capacity, and knowing his face was a grotesque mask and his
> voice a suggestion of drollery. I think it not unlikely with another face
> and voice, Liston might have succeeded in tragedy; but this is only
> saying that, had he been another man, he would have been another
> actor. His mistake lay in not perceiving that with such physical
> qualifications, tragedy was impossible to him.[11]

Lewes, like many other commentators, is carried away, perhaps, by the
romantic notion, perenially popular, of the clown who wants to play
Hamlet. Liston may have hankered after tragedy, but he seems to have
accepted the mantle of low comedian without too much distress.

Whether or not Liston aspired to be a great tragedian, he certainly had
a serious side to his character. His wife, recounting how upset he was by
the news of the death of a friend in India, commented on how his mind
was "always disposed to the melancholy".[12] Westland Marston commented on Liston's kind and sympathetic nature, which was easily
affected at the theatre by a pathetic speech or situation. He once saw
Liston at the Haymarket, weeping copiously at a touching passage in a
play. He sat, said Marston, at the front of the dress-circle, and the tears,
which he made no effort to conceal, streamed down his face.[13] Liston was
certainly prone to fits of depression: Ann Mathews recalled his "generally
pensive habit of mind" and some people found him dull in company.
Hazlitt had reported that Liston felt downcast if the smallest dog failed to
wag its tail in approbation at him. Yet, when asked by Mr. Northcote if
Liston was low-spirited, he replied that Liston could be grave and
prosing, but that there was nothing the matter with him.[14] Both Planché
and Ann Mathews felt there were two sides to Liston. Planché recalled
how, although there was a strong romantic and sentimental side to his
character, Liston's love of fun was great and spilled over into his private
life. In high spirits, said Ann Mathews, Liston was as exuberant as any
boy.[15] He might at times be melancholy, but such rumours were
probably accentuated by the gravity of his appearance: his comic
technique greatly depended on the solemnity of his features and his ability
to keep a straight face in the most absurd circumstances.

After Liston had completed his Haymarket engagement as Baron Wildenheim, Morris offered him very favourable terms to remain for another fortnight. Throughout his engagement he had attracted crowded and fashionable audiences. But Liston declined, alleging his health required a change of air and scenery. Another reason was that he planned to visit Germany at the beginning of September, to place his son at the University of Gottingen. So it was that he left the Haymarket Theatre for the last time, for he never returned to perform there throughout the remainder of his career.

Liston spent the rest of the year at Drury Lane, where he was not altogether happy. He was irritated by the frequency with which Miss Graddon played in the same pieces as he did. She was an actress whose charming manner with her audiences did not totally conceal her innate vulgarity or her lack of technical skill. Liston found her far less congenial than Madame Vestris, Mrs. Humby or Miss Love and was almost ready to give up his engagement on her account. He was also deprived of his wife's company while he was in London, for she had remained at Brighton, where she was fully caught up in the social life. She did not even think she would have time to go up to London until Christmas. Consequently she was unable to follow the sensational sequence of performances which Charles Kemble's daughter, Fanny, had been giving at Covent Garden, since her debut as Juliet in October.[16]

Earlier in the year, while at Drury Lane, Liston had been involved in an altercation with the dramatist, Richard Brindsley Peake. Peake was infuriated when his new play *Master's Rival* was withdrawn after only three performances. He blamed Liston, who failed to bring to life the part of Paul Shack, because, said Peake, he was drunk every night and couldn't remember his lines.[17] When the play was published, Peake included a preface to this effect, but at the time of its performance many of the critics felt sympathetic towards Liston, as usual condemned to bring an under-written part to life.

James Winston recalled another occasion at Drury Lane when Liston's performance was affected by heavy drinking. During a performance of *The Slave*, on 15 May, 1827, Liston was so drunk that he fell asleep in his dressing room and failed to come on in the last scene. His absence caused great confusion on stage and the audience called for him, to no avail. When he appeared in the farce, *Comfortable Lodgings*, there were hisses and cries of "Off! Off!" Liston didn't apologise to them; he merely doffed his hat, but before long his description of the amorous intrigues of the dry-salter's wife had restored the audience to good humour.[18]

Liston did drink heavily on occasion and appeared drunk on stage more than once. It was rumoured that he would often get through a complete bottle of brandy on evenings when he was performing. Dickens, in his essay *The Theatrical Young Gentleman*, stated that:

> Mr. Liston always had a footman in gorgeous livery waiting at the side-scene with a brandy bottle and tumbler, to administer half a pint or so of spirit to him every time he came off, without which assistance he must infallibly have fainted,[19]

although such a story is probably as tall as Dickens means it to sound. Liston was not averse to drink, but there are several hundred plays and several thousand performances about which no charges of drunkeness are made. Compared with the notorious predeliction for drink shown by Cooke, Kean, Emery and Oxberry, Liston was relatively moderate in his habits.

The stresses of an actor's life, however, remained as great as ever and, in 1830, Liston decided to set out on a farewell tour of the provinces. In the spring of the previous year his provincial engagements had ranged from Bristol and Birmingham to Newcastle and Glasgow. He found the journeys very tiring and was eager to forego the rigours of contemporary travel conditions. He had invested wisely and no longer needed to earn such large sums. The provinces, themselves, were not as remunerative as they had been. Post-war inflation had taken its toll and provincial theatres were amongst the victims of declining economic conditions. In announcing a series of farewell visits, Liston would release himself from the obligations of further touring and also attract larger audiences than might otherwise attend.

Early in January, 1830, Liston completed a short provincial tour, visiting Bath and Bristol, then travelling northwards to appear at Liverpool and Preston. From there he returned to Drury Lane, for a short but remunerative engagement. Provincial engagements had to be particularly enticing for Liston to accept them, as he had explained in a letter to Smith, manager of the Norwich Theatre the previous year:

> My London engagement – he wrote – being by the night, with *two* benefits which are insured to produce a specified sum, provided I perform a given number of nights in a given part of the season, renders me very indifferent to a provincial engagement, unless it be so lucrative as to save me from losing any of the above named advantages; I cannot therefore, consistently with prudence, enter into arrangements with you, but upon the terms mentioned in my former letter.[20]

There was not time to visit Norwich in 1830 either, for when he set out on his major tour, which commenced in March, he travelled to Edinburgh, making a brief detour only to appear at Manchester and Chester. On 12 April he appeared for the last time before the Edinburgh public, as Paul Pry, and during the evening delivered a farewell address composed especially for them. Then he proceeded to Glasgow, where he gave his last performance on Scottish soil on 22 April. From Scotland he proceeded south to Newcastle, where he was to take leave of his old friends and patrons. He attracted only middling houses to begin with, but towards the end of his engagement the theatre became more crowded. On his last night there he thanked the audience for their early support of his endeavours:

> It is no mean boast – he said – and I am proud to make it, that whilst the names of George Frederick Cooke and Munden already grace your theatrical annals, you will hereafter have to add the humble name of Liston. It now only remains for me to repeat that painful word, farewell! and conclude by wishing you all, from the bottom of my heart, health and happiness, with prosperity to the town and trade of "Canny New Castle".[21]

After Newcastle, Liston played a few nights at Sunderland, then continued to York. At the York Theatre, recently acquired by a Mr. Butler, attendances were poor during the early part of Liston's engagement, but improved later when competition from the annual village festivals had died down. Liston was unhappy to receive only £94 after four nights of performing.[22] Still, the farewell tour proved quite successful overall and Liston was pleased to be free, at last, of his provincial commitments. In towns large and small, in Scotland, the North of England, the Midlands, the South and West, he had been a welcome and popular visitor.

Although Liston returned to the Drury Lane Theatre during the 1830–31 season, playing Jack Humphries in Poole's new farce *Turning the Tables* and the ridiculous Narcissus Stubble in Ben Webster's *Highways and Byways*, he added nothing new to his reputation. He played regularly, two or three nights a week, for most of the season, largely in old favourites. Times were precarious: the managers of the large patent theatres were rapidly losing money and were continually on the verge of bankruptcy. Liston himself was feeling tired and putting little energy into his performances. He might well have considered an early retirement, if he had not received a request from his old friend, Madame Vestris, to join her in her newly established company at the Olympic Theatre. The terms were too good to refuse: in the autumn of 1831 he did not re-engage at either of the patent theatres, but moved to the Olympic instead. For the next six years his career was to take a relatively new direction.

Pl. 31(a)

Chapter IX

The Olympic Years – 1831–37

Liston is at the Olympic, playing the part of Atlas, and supporting Vestris's fortunes on his broad shoulders. Nightly, since the opening on Saturday week, he has performed in *Talk of the Devil* and, as far as we can see, constituted the main attraction of the house.[1]

Liston had recently made his debut at the Olympic Theatre, as Dominique the Deserter in *Talk of the Devil*, an adaptation from the French by the architect Samuel Beazley. The part was unevenly written, veering uneasily from low comedy and double-entendre to melodramatic bombast and pathos. Even so, Liston must have been surprised by the audience's response when the curtains first drew apart to reveal him on stage on 1 October, 1831. "Who'd have thought it?" he said. The audience roared. "Six months ago who would have looked for such a train of circumstances?" Another roar of laughter greeted this remark. "Yet here I am." An immense roar! The audience took the allusions to apply to Liston's appearance at the Olympic and assumed that he was there because of personal hardship. Liston was disconcerted – the more seriously he tried to keep within the part, the more the audience laughed.

If Liston was startled by his first night reception at the Olympic, he soon settled in and before long was one of the mainstays of Madame Vestris's Company. Vestris had only recently undertaken the management of the Olympic Theatre in Wych Street, commencing her first season in January, 1831. She redecorated the theatre, assembled her own company and commissioned new plays. Since the theatre was not licensed for the presentation of "legitimate" drama, burlettas, extravaganzas and farces were the usual fare – three or four of which would be performed each night. Each piece tended to be of short duration, so that the evening performances were usually over by 11 o'clock. This must have pleased Liston, who had sometimes acted into the small hours of the morning at the patent theatres. Once, when he and his wife were staying at the Ship Hotel in Dover, they were passing through the hall after a walk, when the landlady begged him to come into the parlour and speak to a young lady who wished to renew acquaintance with him. She feared Liston wouldn't recollect her and she was right. The only time they had previously met was when she acted with him in a farce at quarter to one in the morning during the previous season at the Haymarket.[2] At the Olympic, not only did the programme finish at a civilised hour, but new plays tended to run for longer as well. A new piece was usually added to the repertoire about every three weeks and would usually run for well over thirty performances. The high quality of these productions and the elegance of its appearance turned the Olympic into the most fashionable theatre in London during the 1830s. The green-room was the nightly resort of the aristocracy and Count D'Orsay, Lady Blessington and the young Charles Dickens, in the first flush of his fame, were among the theatre's regular patrons.

Vestris was desperately in need of a low comedian; her first season had particularly suffered because of the lack of a suitable performer. Once she had enticed her old Haymarket colleague to join her, at a reputed weekly salary of £60,[3] her success was assured. Like Vestris Liston could draw audiences single-handed and he proved a great asset to the theatre. "Some of Liston's best parts were 'created' at the Olympic", wrote J. M. Langford, "and he was probably never seen to greater advantage than there. His quietest and best manner fitted the house".[4] At last Liston was able to communicate such recognisable emotions as jealousy, fear, anxiety without recourse to the exaggeration required by the large patent houses. In his years with Vestris he created around thirty new roles, an astonishing number considering he was now at an age when most comic actors would have relied on old favourites to maintain their reputation. Vestris fully heeded the value of Liston to her establishment and took great pains to see that he was comfortable there.[5]

Within three weeks of his engagement Liston appeared in another new piece, as Mr. Placid in *I'll Be Your Second*. The author was George Herbert Buonaparte Rodwell, later to be musical director at Covent Garden and a leading campaigner for a national opera house in England. He had recently married Liston's daughter, Emma, a marriage, some suspected, motivated by a desire for self-advancement rather than affection. Liston generously gave them a marriage portion of £20,000,[6] but Emma and Rodwell lived very unhappily together. Although she had two daughters by him, the couple eventually separated. Emma had hoped to make a career on the stage for herself as a singer, but, after an auspicious start, her ailing marriage dampened her enthusiasm. Her brother, John Terry, avoided the pitfalls of marriage: he remained a bachelor and embarked on a career in the army, as an infantry officer.

By the early 1830s Liston had moved back to St. George's Place in Brompton. He lived in one of two low-built houses, with square plate glass windows, adjoining St. George's Hospital. He dressed rather conspicuously, in nankeen trousers and waistcoat, laurel-green coat with gilt buttons, pink hose, shoes with large bows of broad black ribbon, and a white hat. On Sundays, thus attired, he could often be seen on his way to the Chapel Royal in St. James's, where the new King, William IV, had allowed him two sittings. He was often the object of general attention, for not only did he dress ostentatiously, but he always carried a large quarto Prayer-Book, bound in red morocco, under his arm.[7] He collected a large library of books on theological subjects and, despite the attention he attracted on the way to church, it was later said of him that:

> His attention to religion was always marked by no ostentation, but by a devout sincerity; his knowledge of the scriptures was very extensive.[8]

Although he was a devout family man himself, Liston was intrigued by the mess that one of his old Haymarket acquaintances had got herself into. Mrs Humby, the wife of an actor-dentist whom she had married in Hull, had replaced Madame Vestris as Phoebe in *Paul Pry* and played opposite Liston in a number of productions at the Haymarket. She had been so delicate and modest, that she had shrunk from the public gaze and couldn't even bear to have her likeness depicted in prints. Then she had suddenly left her husband for a Mr. Grant, but before long had placed herself under the protection of the notorious Ephraim Bond.* Grant called at Mrs Humby's residence to collect his whip, which he had left there by mistake: Bond was there, standing by the fire-place, and struck Grant in the face. As a result of this fracas Grant followed Mrs Humby's carriage one night to find out where Bond lived and another altercation occurred. Grant had threatened Mrs Humby's life and had said that he would follow her all over London and "do for her" before he left her. The matter came to court and was widely reported in the press. Liston, for some reason, noted down the outcome of the court case on a scrap of paper and then scribbled out the following verse:

> By the lord, you mistake,
> If you think I can't make,
> A rhyme on your name, *Mrs Humby*;
> If exposed to the air,
> Your face, Ma'am, is so fair,
> How white when seen, must your Bum be![9]

*lessee of the Queen's Theatre

Plate 25 Scene from *Paul Pry*

The illustration shows Liston as Paul Pry, Madame Vestris as Phoebe, and William
Farren as Colonel Hardy

Plate 26 Liston and Vestris in the duet of Buy-a-Broom

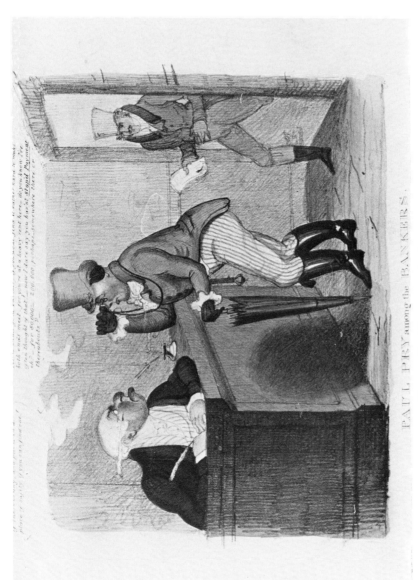

Plate 27 Paul Pry among the Bankers

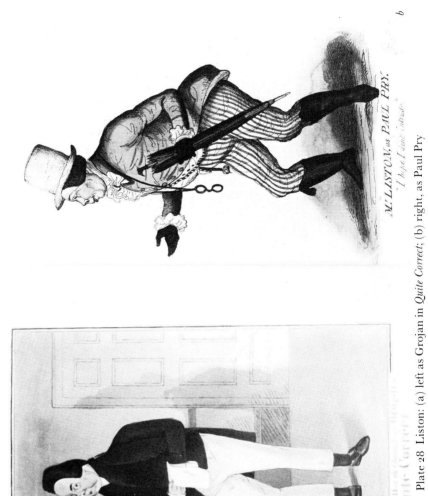

Mr LISTON, as PAUL PRY.

"I hope I don't intrude."

Plate 28 Liston: (a) left as Grojan in *Quite Correct*; (b) right, as Paul Pry

a

b

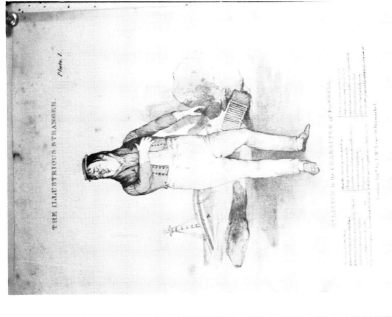

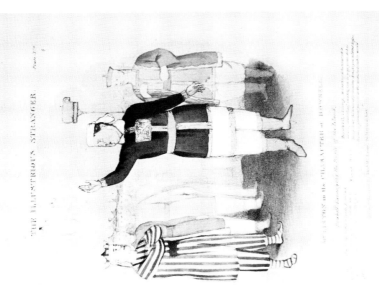

Plate 29 Liston: (a) left and (b) right, as Bowbell in *The Illustrious Stranger*

LISTON AND FARREN.

C. MATHEWS

THE OLD AND YOUNG STAGER.

LISTON

a   b

Plate 30 (a) left, Liston and William Farren in *Charles XII*; (b) right, Liston and Charles Mathews the younger in *The Old and Young Stager*

a

PORTRAIT OF MR. LISTON,

IN THE CHARACTER OF

Mr. Sedley, in " A Gentleman in Difficulties."

b

Plate 31 Liston: (a) left, as Narcissus Stubble in *Highways and Byways*; (b) right, as Mr. Sedley in *A Gentleman in Difficulties*

AS

FIGARO

Price One Penny to the PURCHASERS of No 275 of Figaro in London.

Plate 32 Liston as Figaro in *The Two Figaros*

It was unlikely that the verse originated from Liston, for it was well known at the time and had indirectly contributed to Mrs Humby's notoriety.

The times were difficult, however, for more than Mrs Humby. A cholera epidemic was sweeping through London and there was great political unrest, shortly to lead to the passing of the first great Reform Bill. In such anxious times Londoners found it quite exhilarating to spend an evening in the atmosphere of gaiety, cheerfulness and good humour that pervaded the Olympic Theatre. Liston continued to appear in new roles: as Augustus Galopade, in *The Widow*, an adaptation of *Who Wins*, he recreated his old role of Caper and played opposite Vestris herself. Price Prettyman, in Charles Dance's *He's Not A-Miss*, was another dancing master, most notable for his hair "of the luxuriant cauliflower style of arrangement". In T. H. Bayly's *My Eleventh Day*, as Long Singleton, a jealous old bachelor, he again played opposite Vestris. In all these roles he was highly praised: not a look or tone was lost in the small Olympic auditorium and many critics admired the detail with which he invested each part.

There was one weak performance, at the end of the season, when Liston · undertook the absurd role of Von Noodle in *The Young Hopefuls*, a rather indifferent play by John Poole. Vestris had written to Poole as soon as she had engaged Liston, suggesting that he create a new character for the comedian to play.[10] Liston's casual attitude to the part infuriated Poole, who wrote a strong letter to the *Morning Chronicle*, accusing Liston of being too drunk to play the part properly and of imperfectly remembering his lines. He said that Liston had ruined his property by his behaviour and vowed that he would never write another part for him.[11] Liston remained aloof from this attack, but the *Athenaeum* (17/3/1832) took up his defence, stating that Poole's allegations, as far as it was concerned, were not borne out by the performances of the play it had witnessed. Indeed, the blame may have been partly Poole's, for Von Noodle was one of the worst and most underwritten roles to come Liston's way for a long time. If Liston put little effort into the performance of it, Poole had only himself to blame – the play had little to commend it and Madame Vestris withdrew it, not surprisingly, after two performances.

Neither Kenney nor Poole, both of whom had provided Liston with some of his best parts, wrote anything very memorable for the Olympic. The sort of burlettas preferred by Vestris were more competently produced by such dramatists as T. H. Bayly, Charles Dance and J. R. Planché. Planché and Dance also created many of the extravaganzas for which the Olympic was so famous, although Liston never appeared in any of these. Liston was increasingly playing more subdued, middle-class characters, jealous husbands, old bachelors and cowardly suitors, in the domestic pieces written by Vestris's new playwrights. In many of these plays, including *The Water Party, Kill or Cure* and *Forty and Fifty*, he played opposite Mary Ann Orger, a clever and highly cultivated woman, whose restrained performances in domestic roles made her a firm favourite with the Olympic public. Liston, himself, was praised for his "quiet, subdued style of natural acting"[12] in these plays, which in tone are similar to the short stories of domestic life that Dickens published in *Sketches By Boz*.[13] He obviously conformed to the innovations in acting style that Madame Vestris imposed upon her company, even though this led spectators like Crabb Robinson to assume that he was no longer "the very comic creature that he was".[14] With age Liston had grown fat, and looked much graver – "the flexibility of his humorous countenance", noted Macready, when he met Liston walking along the promenade at Brighton in the summer of 1833, "seems to stiffen under the chill of age".[15]

During the 1832–33 season Liston had been taken ill several times. Since his Covent Garden days he had been prone to ill health and his absences from the theatre due to illness were frequent enough to suggest that he possibly suffered from hypochondria or from some nervous disorder that prevented him acting. Whatever the cause, he was absent from the Olympic for most of December, 1832, and when he returned in *Kill or Cure* on 31 December he was advertised as "newly recovered from his late, severe indisposition". He cannot have been fully recovered, for a couple of weeks later, while Madame Vestris was singing one of her songs in *My Eleventh Day*, he suddenly floundered in a chair at the back of the stage. When Vestris had finished singing, the prompter gave Liston's cue, but to no avail, for he was completely insensible. Two doctors were called and, for a time, the worst was feared. The curtain was dropped and all was confusion behind the scenes. Vestris was dreadfully shocked and had hysterics as Liston was carried out. Although one letter in the press suggested that Liston's illness was no more than the after-effects of heavy drinking,[16] it was generally reported that Liston's attack was so severe that he was thinking of giving up his engagement and had asked Madame Vestris to release him from his contract.[17] According to one witness:

> The fogs of London do not agree with Liston, who seriously thinks of giving up his engagement at the Olympic. He has for some weeks taken every measure to preserve his health. He has invariably gone to the theatre in a closed carriage, his head encased in a velvet night-cap, which, with the addition of a *large shawl, bon* and *muff*, made him look a most interesting personage.[18]

The new piece which Liston had been rehearsing, *All's Right*, a play by Planché first performed at the Haymarket in 1827, was almost cancelled.

Liston's illness had so frequently prevented its performance, wrote one of the Olympic actresses to a friend, that Madame Vestris feared its title was ominous of the contrary.[19] By 21 January, however, Liston had recovered sufficiently to re-appear:

> *All's Right*, or nearly so, at the Olympic. Liston again appeared, and though not quite recovered from the effects of his late illness, we see little reason to apprehend a relapse, provided he is tolerably *prudent*, and takes care of himself. This he is bound to do; he should consider his consequence to the public. We could dispense with half the House of Commons, a third of the Judges, nine tenths of the peers and the whole bench of Bishops, with less loss of enjoyment than we should experience in the absence of *Paul Pry*. His departure would cause a gap in our state not to be repaired. Liston is himself alone; there are actors of higher talent, of greater versatility, of more extensive accomplishments, but there is not one who has his faculty of so appropriating a character that none after him shall be tolerated in it. He has a prerogative of royalty – whatever piece he stamps his phiz upon is current without question; all imitations are counterfeit.[20]

As the bumptious, familiar Mr. Cool Liston gave a performance that was praised because:

> No actor but Liston – the impenetrable gravity of whose countenance is so remarkable – could make anything of such a character; he, however, renders it a complete and perfect study – a little bit of life so like reality, that one does not hesitate to consider it an everyday acquaintance. There is no caricature nor grimace about his performance.[21]

Such a review was typical of Liston's years at the Olympic – he turned in restrained, credible performances in play after play, very much in keeping with the more realistic style of acting that Vestris was trying to foster.

Liston usually acted for the duration of the Olympic season, which lasted through from the autumn to the spring of the following year, but he rarely undertook other engagements now. It was reported that he had been engaged to act with a company at Hythe in Kent in July, 1832, but the Mayor refused to grant the manager of the Hythe Theatre permission to perform and, when he found he had been disobeyed, sent constables in to demand a £50 fine and to confiscate the scenery.[22] In 1833 he appeared gratis at the Olympic for a couple of nights, to support the destitute Covent Garden company which had moved there. Laporte, who was then Manager at Covent Garden, had gone bankrupt, but his company negotiated the use of the Olympic for the last few months of the season, in order to avoid the hardship threatened by the early closure of Covent Garden.

The following season Alfred Bunn took over the management of Covent Garden; he was already manager of Drury Lane, so that he now had control over both of the large patent theatres. In 1834 he negotiated with Liston to play for him for a few weeks at the end of the season. Bunn was not the most engaging of men; indeed, he was once so aggravating to Macready that the tragedian actually struck him. Bunn found Liston difficult, for every new part he sent to him, Liston rejected. He turned down Kenney's *A Goodlooking Fellow*, feared J. B. Buckstone's new farce was "a barrel of gunpowder" and declined the part of Mr. Narcissus Briggs, especially concocted for him by Kenney and Bunn. He preferred, instead, a quieter farce by Charles Dance, entitled *Pleasant Dreams*. Bunn was infuriated by this obtuseness: as far as he was concerned, Liston was just using his reputation to be difficult. In fact, Liston probably preferred Dance's farce, in that it was less grotesque and more in line with the pieces in which he was now playing at the Olympic Theatre. As for choice of role, that had been his prerogative for many years and a normal practice among "star" actors.

Bunn was even more annoyed by Liston's attitude, when requested to play at a Royal Command Performance that was to take place at Covent Garden on 1 May. He was grudgingly paying Liston twenty pounds to appear in *Turning the Tables* for this event, but two days before the performance he was infuriated to receive the following note from the comedian:

> I perceive by the advertisements that *Turning the Tables* is to be performed as the last piece on Thursday next; this I trust will not be persisted in, otherwise I must decline the honour of appearing before his majesty so late in the evening.[23]

"Now pray who is the KING in all this business?" expostulated Bunn. If it wasn't too late for the King of England to sit in his private box, how could it be too late for one of "his majesty's servants" to entertain him! Still, he approached the Lord Chamberlain, who allowed the "nonsensical alteration" to be made.

Bunn suspected that Liston's refusal was because he was afraid that William IV would be too tired to find him amusing, after laughing heartily at all the preceding pieces. He was amused on the night of the command performance, when he stood with Liston in the ante-room of the royal box, conversing with a nobleman attached to the royal household. A

THE OLYMPIC YEARS – 1831–1837

page passed by who, not seeing the nobleman, slapped Liston on the back and said, "D'ye think you'll make him laugh tonight? He was devillishly stupid at dinner". Bunn could not determine which was the funnier – the face of Liston or the face of the page on perceiving the nobleman:

> If the reader never saw the face of a dignified performer, when reminded that he was nothing more *than* a performer, he has a treat to come.[24]

In the event Liston's performance was so successful on 1 May that he repeated it again the following evening. Three weeks later he commenced a month's engagement at Covent Garden. Oliver Sanguine in *Pleasant Dreams* proved a little too restrained for so large a theatre, but Baillie Jarvie and Moll Flaggon proved as popular as ever. Other old parts were revived for benefits, including Mawworm, Neddy Bray and Adam Brock. For Bunn's benefit, at Drury Lane, Liston played one of his Olympic parts, Brown in *Kill or Cure*.

Back at the Olympic in the autumn, Liston continued to play his usual range of jealous husbands, unsuitable suitors and inveterate cowards. Often he was paired with Robert Keeley, another quiet comedian: usually they were rivals in love, as in *Hush Money* or *Fighting by Proxy*.[25] It was during this season that the County D'Orsay, one of the Olympic's most fashionable patrons, was surprised to receive a strange request from his tailor. He was asked to authorise an order for a coat identical to the highly distinctive garment that he always wore. Thinking that some admiring friend sought to emulate him, the Count gave his permission and thought no more about it. A few days later, when he visited the new play at the Olympic, he was amazed to see Liston on stage, wearing the very coat he had authorised. He was highly amused by Liston's imitation of him and soon *The Retort Courteous*, with Liston "hitting off the Count's appearance to a hair" as Icarus Hawk, became the sensation of the fashionable world. The private boxes were nightly filled with members of the *haut ton*, who not only delighted in Liston's performance, but also in a tableau vivant at the end of the first act, with Madame Vestris costumed elaborately as Queen Elizabeth I and Liston impersonating the Earl of Leicester. A further treat was the revival of the grotesque broom-girl dance, which was somehow woven into the play.[26]

Two of the highlights of the 1834–35 season were *How to Get Off*, in which a travelling carriage was drawn on stage by three horses, with Liston as Mr. Dulcimer seated on top of the coach and Madame Vestris seated inside, and *A Scene of Confusion*. In the second play Liston was the jealous husband of an actress making her debut at the Olympic Theatre and kept interrupting the action from one of the side-boxes. He is so incensed when he discovers that his wife has to be kissed by the leading man that he climbs onto the stage and insists on taking over the main part. Before the audience realised that the interruptions came from Liston, all was literally confusion in the auditorium for a short while.

The year 1835 was overshadowed, however, by the death of Liston's old friend Charles Mathews. After a fatiguing visit to America, he had returned to England in very ill health and passed away in Plymouth on 28 June. Liston had always been a close family friend, taking an interest in Mathews' son, Charles James, whom he had helped out on a number of occasions. The younger Mathews had written several plays: one of them, *Pong Wong*, had been performed at the Haymarket in 1826, with Liston in the title role, but it had not been well received. In 1831 Liston recommended another play by Mathews, *Pyramus and Thisbe*, to Madame Vestris, who agreed to put it on, although nothing came of her decision. After his father's death Mathews decided to take up acting professionally and it was to the Olympic, with its freedom from the more laboured and more conventional forms of theatrical presentation, that he turned.

Liston was probably responsible for introducing the young Mathews to Vestris. She lacked a good light comedy actor, so she eagerly engaged Mathews, who possessed the elegance and lightness of touch required in that particular line. His debut was fixed for the 7 December, 1835: he was to play in one of his own pieces, *The Humpback'd Lover*, and to be teamed with Liston in a new play especially written for the occasion by William Leman Rede, *The Old and Young Stager*. Liston also agreed to introduce the son of his old friend to the London public in a specially devised prologue. News of Mathews' debut drew a very large and fashionable audience to the theatre. From the very hour when it had been announced, there had been a rush to the box office to secure places. On the night of the debut Wych Street was invaded by a galaxy of rank and fashion, members of both houses of Parliament, well-known actors and actresses, all of whom were crammed into every nook and cranny of the little Olympic auditorium.

The curtain at last drew back to reveal Liston, standing by a chair in the centre of the stage, handkerchief in hand, ready to deliver the introductory address. The first two lines:

> Oh let me beg – this night – with you – and *here*,
> One moment to be serious – and sincere.

had the reverse of the effect intended. The more serious Liston appeared, the more the audience laughed. As he dwelt on memories of the father, at times close to tears, the audience quietened. By the time he had concluded the address, which many thought he spoke very beautifully, he was heartily applauded. The introduction of Charles Mathews the younger had been effected.

The highlight of the evening was *The Old and Young Stager*, in which   *Pl. 30(b)*
Liston played an old coachman, Tim Topple, a respectable conservative stager of the old school. Mathews played his son, Tom, a lively young "tiger". Liston bore himself with magnificent pomposity – "he looked as full-blown as the flowers at his button-hole".[27] When the curtains drew to reveal Liston and Mathews at work in the stable-yard, the applause was immense. In the midst of this reception Liston took Mathews by the hand and led him forwards to the footlights, which, of course, intensified the volume of applause even more. Many remembered the strange appearance of the two men, as they stood there together:

> The elder comedian, with his elongated face, his solemn self-complacency of look and manner, and his oracular voice, was the model of a stage dignitary, with well-defined features, florid complexion and light, wavy hair. Charles Mathews, in his arch, easy gaiety, toned down by respect to Liston, was to some extent, as the stage novice, a sort of aristocratic prototype of Sam Weller.[28]

When the play at last began, the audience was delighted with the wealth of theatrical allusion it contained. The pace of the dialogue between the old and young stager was fast and furious. Topple began by telling his son he was uneasy on his account.

"Are you though!" replied Tom. Then, in an aside to the audience, he added, "It's more than I am on my own account".

"Yes I am" continued Topple. "You're just entering into life, and don't know what you've got to go through; it's my duty to tell you". He then elaborated: "If ever you hope to reach the dignity I have – to be as high as I am – you must do as I have done".

"I'm sure I wish for nothing better than to do as you have done", replied Tom. "If everyone as he comes to the end of his journey could see, as you do, the prospect of a good inn and a hearty welcome, there would be little to complain of".

Topple then told his son how he himself had first become a coachman:

"I went by regular steps, stable boy, groom, 'till I drove a market cart, then a shay cart, then a stage in the country, then, after some time, I took the stage up to town".

Tom asked his father about these early experiences:

"Aye, and when you first topp'd the stage, you must have felt awkward; it's a trying thing to a young hand. How did you get on?"

"As nice as ninepence; I was *Sheepfaced* at first, trying it though, but when I first came to town, the stages were very different to what they are now".

"Aye, so I've heard".

"Bless your soul, driven by regular, steady hands. Talk of stages! There was old Tom Harris; he drove the National; what a concern there was, all full inside! There was an opposition stage at the same time; but all full fare, no reductions. That was Dick Sherry's. That was a good concern too, for Sherry always made friends with his *Rivals*".

"How came these concerns to break up, then?"

"Why", said old Topple, referring of course to the decline of the patent theatres, "all the best horses grew old; some went to paddock in plenty, some fell away; the coachmen one by one dropped off; the guards were discontinued, the reins were taken into strange hands; the stage was made to carry beasts instead of men, 'till the poor old 'National' became a mere 'Spectacle' at last".

Tom then put the modern viewpoint:

"Ah! these old affairs were very well, but what prime light things our modern stages are. Carry a proper number of passengers and no heavy luggage – make four short stages, and always get to the end of a day's journey in good time; it's quite a treat to secure the box seat – there are your lamps in front, the guard playing, the passengers merry, and nothing but laugh and gig the whole of the way".

The audience was delighted with the dialogue, fully grasping the implied contrast between the patent theatres and the policy of the Olympic Theatre. At the end of the play, when Tom has promised to mend his ways, Liston as Old Topple spoke the final lines of the play:

"There then, and may you live as long in this family and with as much mutual satisfaction, as I have. And now Tom, let me give you a bit of advice. You are entering a new line of life, a stranger to the road – I know it well, it has its errors and its accidents – but you reach the Inn at last; and I believe there's no-one here need be asked twice to "remember the coachman". Passengers we leave you here – as he carries on the stage, be his guard, he's my boy, and if he don't always handle the whip like an old hand – make allowances, for the sake of his father".

Liston's final tag virtually brought down the house and moved many of the audience to tears. Mathews and Liston appeared deeply moved as the old comedian led forward his protegée by the hand and hinted that, in return for so much applause, Mathews should take a long bow. The interest he had taken in his friend's son had been almost paternal and, now and again, there had been a touch of tenderness, a break in his voice, which showed that he had been thinking of former days. When the curtains closed, he was so overcome that he sank into an armchair on the stage and remained there for a long time, too drained to do anything. Mathews, meanwhile, was surrounded by admirers, among them some of the most distinguished men of the day. His debut, so ably assisted by Liston's exertions, had proved a triumph.

By the autumn of 1836 Liston was feeling ill and out of spirits. From his country house in Penn, Buckinghamshire, where he now spent a lot of time, he wrote declining the part of the Duke of Abbemarle in Planché's new comedy, *Court Favour* and begged to be released from his engagement.[29] In the end he returned to the Olympic, appearing for the first time on 29 September, but it was to prove his last season. His most memorable new role was Figaro in an adept pastiche by Planché of *The Marriage of Figaro* and *The Barber of Seville*: it took up the adventures of the Beaumarchais characters sixteen years later, being, in effect, a sort of "Son of Figaro". Vestris, Mathews and Liston proved a good ensemble in this production, which provided the audience with "a combination of talent seldom witnessed".[30] "Notwithstanding the age of Liston", noted Crabb Robinson, "and the evident decline of his powers not of mind but body, he and Mathews made good fun in *The Two Figaros*.[31]   *Pl. 32*

One comic moment came at the end of the play, when Liston had to speak two well-known lines of Pope as a tag:

> If to my share some human failings fall,
> Look in my face, and you'll forget them all.

When Liston came forward and spoke the first line, the Olympic audience, conscious of Liston's face and of the line that was to follow, burst into a roar of laughter, which lasted several minutes. Liston did not move a muscle or attempt to continue, until quiet was restored. Then, gravely and correctly, as if there was nothing funny in the lines, he completed the tag to renewed mirth. J. M. Langford considered this a good instance of Liston's "stolidity" – "his perfect immobility in the most ridiculous situations".[32]

Liston fell ill several times during the season, but he was as fit as ever by its conclusion. The previous year there had been doubts as to whether Liston would continue to act. Now he was determined to retire, although many were surprised when Madame Vestris failed to announce his farewell performance in her playbills. It was rumoured that he was negotiating for the use of one of the large patent theatres for his last public appearance, but a later report stated that his nerves were in such a weak

state that it was impossible for him to take a formal farewell. He apparently dreaded being called upon by the audience and it was thought that the painful ceremony of leave-taking would probably be dispensed with.[33] On 31 May, 1837, he took his leave of the Olympic Theatre as Monsieur Champignon, a vain and amorous grocer, in Planché's *A*
Pl. 31 (b)   *Peculiar Position* and as the jealously perplexed Mr. Sedley in Bayly's *A Gentleman in Difficulties*. At the end of the evening Liston was loudly called for by the audience, who understood this to be his last performance at the Olympic. Vining, the stage manager, stepped forward and assured the audience that Liston would be acting again at Covent Garden in the following weeks. He then added:

> But should you, Ladies and Gentlemen, merely wish to bestow upon him your testimonials of present approbation, he is perfectly ready to appear before you.[34]

The audience vociferously demonstrated their assent and Vining soon reappeared, leading Liston by the hand. Liston repeatedly bowed his thanks, with his hand on his heart, then retired. On 2 June he played Champignon for his son-in-law Rodwell's benefit at Covent Garden, a role he repeated a week later for Charles Mathews' benefit at the same theatre. On Saturday 10 June he made his final professional appearance on any stage, at the Lyceum Theatre, for the benefit of his Olympic colleague, James Vining. Again, his part was Champignon.

Liston retired quietly from the stage, without a formal farewell. His six year association with the Olympic ended as various transformations were occurring there. Vestris's private life was in disarray: during the last weeks of the season she had been involved in bankruptcy proceedings; there were also rumours that she and Charles Mathews had entered into a liaison. Liston was perhaps glad that he was at last quitting the stage for ever, although while at the Olympic he had been second in popularity only to Vestris and, latterly, the younger Mathews. His presence had helped the theatre not only financially but artistically as well. Many critics referred to his restrained, unexaggerated, "natural" style of acting at the Olympic and to his ability to make even the absurdest creation credible. Paradoxically Liston might seem to be one of the most unlikely actors to be found in an establishment largely devoted to theatrical reform. Yet, rather than appearing out of place in the company, he helped to make the Olympic under Vestris one of the most significant theatrical ventures of the early nineteenth century.[35]

Chapter X

Liston in Retirement – 1837–46

Not long after Liston had retired, Ben Webster received a note from him, authorising him to select any six wigs from his stock, which was stored in the Strand, since he wouldn't be using them again. Even though such a gesture implied he had left the stage for good, not everyone was prepared to believe his decision to retire was final. Robert Keeley might say that, of all the men he knew, Liston had had enough of the stage to tire him of it[1], but all the major theatres wanted him back. William Macready, who had just taken over the management of Covent Garden Theatre, made a special journey to Liston's country villa in Penn, near Windsor, to try to persuade him out of retirement. "Arriving at Penn", recounted Macready, "I drove up to Liston's house and found that he had gone to church; I was glad of the opportunity, and, going in, was shown into a pew. The service was most respectably performed, the church very clean and neat ... After the service I looked about the churchyard for Liston, whom I had observed attending very gravely to his duty in church, and when I approached him, his surprise was extreme. I walked home with him, and saw Mrs. Liston and another lady; talked for some time, lunched, and walked out with Liston to look at Taylor's house and see something of the country, which is pretty, but not comparable to the neighbourhood of Elstree. We talked of many things, chiefly theatrical, and I asked him to come to Covent Garden. He said that he never intended to act again. I did not urge him, but as we talked on, I told him we should not differ on terms, and that I should be happy to see him, and would make him as comfortable as I could. I got a frequent repetition of the promise from him that, if he acted anywhere, it should be with me, and I thought I perceived a disposition in him to yield, which I thought it better not to press. Met Taylors, declined their invitations to dinner, and left them on Liston's premises".[2]

Another manager anxious for Liston's services was Alfred Bunn, who still remained lessee of Drury Lane Theatre. He wrote in September to

Liston, who declined his offer, reasserting his decision never to appear again on stage.[3] Macready was no more successful, when he made a second attempt to entice Liston back in October. He called at Liston's town house in Brompton late one morning and sat talking with him for some time. Once more Liston strongly asserted that he would never act again and Macready, who felt Liston seemed to be breaking up, was convinced that he meant it. He left Liston with the expression that he had "carte-blanche" from him.[4]

Although Liston never again appeared on stage, reports of his impending appearance continued to circulate. The Olympic, it was rumoured, was eager to have him back, to compensate for the absence of Vestris and Mathews in America. Even the Haymarket tried to secure his services and, at the beginning of each season, the London theatres often announced the likelihood that he would be engaged. Nothing, however, could lure him back: his health was declining and he was growing more feeble. Macready met him twice in 1838: once in May, when Liston appeared drunk in the Covent Garden green-room; again in November, when Macready was visited by Liston – "old and rickety" – to ask for a friend's name to be added to his wife's on the free list.[5]

The following year Liston was in better spirits, dining out with and borrowing books from such old friends as Ann Mathews and the Planchés. Ann Mathews even tried to persuade Liston to return to the stage to support her son and Madame Vestris, when they assumed from Macready the management of Covent Garden Theatre. Mathews wrote to him, promising that he would be "King of Covent Garden" if he joined them:

> act when you please, what you please, and as long as you please; stop when you please, take what money you please, do what you please and say what you please, and be sure that whatever you please, you cannot fail to please. More than this I cannot add, except that you shall be allowed to sweeten your own tea, and when you are too late for rehearsal, you shall beat the prompter. In plain English, and in sober earnest, if you will at any time make up your mind to gratify us by playing a few of your old parts, everything that mortals can do to make you comfortable and happy shall be done. ...[6]

Liston was touched to receive this letter, which recalled their friendly association of a few years previously, but he remained adamant in his decision not to return to the stage. He claimed that to resume "the cap and bells" at his advanced age would be a moral indecorum and feared the exertion required would probably kill him.[7]

Liston withdrew more and more into private life. William IV had died in 1837 and the accession of Queen Victoria heralded a more sombre and less boisterous mood than before. Liston grew duller and his sense of humour began to desert him. Years before he had loved to play practical jokes, sometimes attracting a lot of public attention when he did so. For instance, he was once passing though Leicester Square in company with Miller the bookseller, talking with vigour about a dainty dinner of stewed tripe he was about to have.

"Beastly stuff!" said Miller
Liston stopped and cried in a loud voice:
"What? You don't like tripe?"
"No!"
"You don't like tripe!" Liston roared again.
People began to look round and stare.
"Hush, for heaven's sake, don't speak so loud", begged Miller. But instead of heeding him, Liston turned to the passers-by and, pointing at Miller, cried:
"There's a man who doesn't like tripe!"
A crowd began to gather and Miller took to his heels, while Liston's cry rang in his ears:
"There goes the man who doesn't like tripe!"[8]

Once, at a Theatrical Fund Dinner, Liston played a prank on an old gentleman, a frequenter of such occasions, who was famed for incessantly repeating the same story. During the evening, Liston slipped out of the room and disguised himself in oriental costume. He was then announced as the Persian Ambassador, who was supposedly attending the dinner especially to hear the old man's story. Liston appeared in silk and paste-beard and wig, bearing his figure with a comic and ferocious dignity. Once the story had been told and the "Ambassador" departed, Liston returned to the room, saying to the old gentleman:
"I am delighted, Sir, that you rendered the story so effective to a person so particularly ignorant of the language".
"Yes", replied the victim, "and so particularly *ugly*, Mr. Liston".[9]
Although not devoid of a sense of humour, Liston generally took himself seriously. In business matters and in social gatherings he proved most adept and he was very much the gentleman when not on stage. He dressed very fashionably and, as his portraits reveal, to his best advantage. He tended to wear high collars, in order to give shape to his otherwise lugubrious features and his hair was often as ornately dressed as the Prince Regent's. Mrs. Egerton, the actress, told a story about Liston's vanity in regard to his appearance:

Pl. 1

Liston – she said – was somewhat personally conceited, and thought, innately, that both his talents and his looks were mistaken by the public. One day having to enact Mawworm in a country theatre, and finding that he had left his character wig behind him, he sent for the only barber in the place, and gave him another wig to do up. When the man returned, he had transformed the wig into a profusion of well-macassared curls. "How is this?" cried Liston, surprised. "Why have you not made the hair fall back smooth and stiffly, combed back as I directed?" "It woun't ha bin the laste proper", answered the barber, eyeing his work in a perfect trance of admiration! "It woun't have done no good to your countenace". "Ah", said Liston, smirking, "then you think the curls become me?" "Sartanly", was the not very agreeable reply, "sartanly; they *hides* your face, an' the more you combs 'em over, the better!"[10]

Now, in solemn old age, Liston began to show an increasing pre-occupation with his poor health. This was not the only thing to trouble him. A particular source of grief to the aged Listons was the unhappy marriage of their daughter, which had led to her separation from Rodwell, her husband.[11] Webster recalls that both of Liston's children had a predilection for the stage, but that their father strongly opposed such an inclination. Liston's son, he said, had performed as an amateur in his father's line of parts, whilst stationed in Jamaica, and had proved quite a hit.[12] In 1838, whilst stationed at Guernsey, a Captain in the eighth regiment of foot, he obtained his Company by purchase, presumably aided by his father.[13]

Although he had a villa in Penn, Liston spent his last years in London, at his house in St. George's Place, near Hyde Park Corner. Here he gradually developed a chronic nervous disease and lost much of his enthusiasm and interest in life. He used to sit at a window all day long, with a stop watch in hand, timing the horse-drawn omnibuses as they went past. This became such an obsession that he would grow very angry if a bus were late. When his old friend Planché called on him, he was shocked at the way Liston's spirits had completely deserted him. "He never smiled or entered into conversation", said Planché, "and eventually sunk into a lethargy from which he awoke no more in this world".[14]

From about 1842 onwards Liston suffered frequent attacks of apoplexy. Nevertheless, despite these attacks and his loss of spirits, he still ventured out occasionally. His last visit to the theatre, in 1846, was to see the Miss Cushmans in *Romeo and Juliet* at the Haymarket. The following day he sent to J. B. Buckstone, the actor-playwright, the manuscript sermon, as delivered by him in the character of Mawworm, together with the shoe buckles he had been accustomed to wear in the part.[15] Shortly after dinner, on Monday 16 March, without any warning, he suffered a severe apoplectic fit, after which he never spoke again. His regular medical attendant, Dr. Cuming of Lowndes Street, assisted by Dr. Mackintyre and Mr. Robert Liston, the eminent surgeon, did all they could to save his life, but in vain. On the morning of Sunday 22 March, his 39th wedding anniversary, Liston died in the arms of his wife.[16]

On the morning of Monday 30 March, at quarter to ten, Liston's remains were buried at Kensal Green cemetery. The funeral was a relatively private affair; there were three mourning carriages, the first of which included Captain John Terry Liston, Planché and Charles Kemble, who appeared much moved at the death of his old friend.[17]

Obituaries duly appeared. One of the most telling was that in the *Athenaeum* (28/3/46):

> The mere announcement itself expresses the sum of all particulars, – the name includes all of the person that the public needs to know. The actor was every man's acquaintance. We should no more think of offering to our readers an account of who Liston was, than of describing the figure of some familiar joke which was in all men's mouths, or by analyzing the laughter that he has rung by every hearth. It is sufficient to say that, for the public whose enjoyment of Liston was once almost a passion, that his place will never be precisely filled up.

In his will Liston left property to the value of £40,000. His plate, jewellery, books, furniture, horses and carriage were left to his wife and the residue of his property was to be invested for her. He left £6,000 to his daughter, the principal of which would succeed to his grand-daughters, Emma and Elizabeth, on their mother's death. The property left to Sarah Liston would succeed to her offspring when she died.[18] In his lifetime Liston had invested wisely, securing independence from financial worry. "He constantly saved money", stated the *Gentleman's Magazine*, "and never but once sold out of funds, and even regularly brought in with the dividends upon his gradual accumulations. Thus he was never in want of money, and never engaged in any questionable speculation".[19] Consequently, Sarah Liston was able to live in relative prosperity until her death, eight years later, in 1854. The year of her death also marked that of her son, still a bachelor, and of her son-in-law.[20]

Despite the publicity surrounding his extraordinary career, Liston kept his private life well hidden. As a result he remains something of an enigma and there is no clear answer to some of the paradoxes that he seems to embody. Reserved in disposition, he was capable of close and affectionate friendships – Bannister he addressed as his dear Papa, Mathews was his big brother. A gentleman in private life, he excelled in portraying familiar and vulgar characters from low life on the stage. Fond of theology and prone to depression, he also possessed an indomitable sense of fun. Interested in serious literature and allegedly desirous of shining in tragedy, his professional life was devoted to the furtherance of ephemeral farces and comedies. One account of Liston hints at this paradox – at the incongruity between the private man and the public actor. It serves, perhaps, as an appropriate epitaph for the man who was undoubtedly the greatest comic actor of his era:

He might be, when alone, as grave and solemn as he chose; he might love tragedy and detest farce; but as a professional man he *must* play the buffoon and, above all, he must make himself ridiculous. There was considerable thought of mind required for this. For it was not the droll character in this or that farce that made people roar and go into fits of laughter. The same droll character might be played with the most exquisite correctness by another artist, and 'twould be comparably insipid. It was absolutely with Liston *himself*, as the ugliest, most awkward, most unlucky and ridiculous of men, that the public were enchanted. To an inferior mind this would have been galling. He knew it, however, and endured it with the fortitude of a hero. Yet his magnanimity did not hinder him from feeling. And it was exactly this feeling, as it were of his own degradation, the droll discomfiture and amazement not merely at cross occurrences in the scene, but that he himself should have turned into a mere buffoon, which, when expressed by Liston, delighted the audience beyond all bounds.[21]

Chapter XI

Liston the Actor

Why was John Liston the greatest comic actor of his generation? What made him so unique among his contemporaries? Why did he achieve so close a rapport with his audiences? Why did he earn more money than any other comic actor of that period? Why did audiences never tire of him in the thirty odd years he played before them? Why is he considered by theatre historians to be the greatest low comedian of the age? The answer to these questions lies, of course, in his technique as an actor and in those qualities which distinguished him from others of his profession. It is to the acting of John Liston that we now must turn in order to assess his extraordinary appeal.

Like many low comedians in the early nineteenth century Liston progressed through a range of low comedy parts. He commenced his London career in country roles, in which fatuity, astonishment, vacancy of mind and utter stupidity seemed to be the predominant features. From these he graduated to affected, boorish characters from the provinces, small townsmen whose vanity, pomposity and vulgarity create a ludicrous portrait of the pettiness of human nature:

> It is in the description of characters where ignorance, worked up with ideas of greatness and the assuming the man of importance, that Liston has no equal. The natural colouring that he gives to persons of this cast is so admirable – his awkward gait – his unpolished manner – his embarrassments – and again – the satisfaction with which he repeats his vulgarities. ... [1]

This sort of character was one of Liston's original contributions to the stage; when a cockney accent was added, as with Log, Billy Lackaday or Fogrun, it became even more popular, exposing as it did the affected consequence of the regency cockney. Later, in more restrained and domestic roles, Liston demonstrated that he could go beyond caricature

99

and excess, especially in the jealous old bachelors and cowardly suitors that he played at the Olympic.

It is clear that a part of the appeal of Liston's characters was the "humours" with which they were invested. They tended to have one over-riding characteristic, whether it be the curiosity of Paul Pry, the stupidity of Van Dunder, the selfishness of Tristram Sappy or the sentimentality of Billy Lackaday. The behaviour and, sometimes, the preoccupations of these characters are obsessive. Often these obsessions or traits recur in a number of plays. Thus many of Liston's characters are conceived, especially as regards their attractions for the opposite sex, from Caper (1808) to Monsieur Champignon (1837), not to mention Apollo Belvi, Narcissus Stubble or Price Prettyman. Interestingly, the predominant humour of a character is often implied in his name, as in the last two examples. Cowardice is another frequent trait, to be found in Memmo in M. G. Lewis's *Rugantino* (1805), Bottom, Bob Acres, Sir Andrew Aguecheek or Jasper Touchwood in *Hush Money* (1833), in which Liston gave "the most ludicrous picture of fear and trepidation that can be imagined".[2] At the Olympic he provided some well-observed portraits of jealousy, including Septimus Lovebond in *Look at Home*:

> The awful mystery of his insinuation, – his unspeakable superiority of manner, – his scarcely concealed pride of delight at the humility of Mrs. Septimus – were the highest taste of true humour.[3]

In these roles Liston evidently presented a shrewd and accurate idea of the weakness of human nature.

As a popular actor, on good terms with his audience, Liston might be expected to play largely sympathetic parts or at least to embody characteristics that were not downright unpleasant. Some characters, like Billy Lackaday, were ludicrously sympathetic; others, such as Adam Brock, Sir Hiliary Heartease in *Roses and Thorns* or Fluid in *The Water Party* were likeable for their evident good nature. Yet a number of Liston's parts involved the portrayal of very unpleasant people: Sam Swipes, Mawworm and Tristram Sappy are all extremely unlikeable, if rather exaggerated in conception; so are the less extremely depicted Janus in *Snakes in the Grass* or Brown in *Kill or Cure*. One of the paradoxes of Liston's career is the way he became so popular playing so many unpleasant roles.

Liston's success in making such characters palatable to his audiences lay in the detail and observation with which he brought them to life. His skill as a comic actor lay partly in his attention to the minutiae which turned his characters into credible beings. This is why he was so highly praised for his performances in smaller theatres, such as the Olympic and the Haymarket. Also, when theatres became better illuminated through the use of gas lighting during the second decade of the nineteenth century, Liston could be seen to better advantage. Unlike Munden or Grimaldi, who pandered to the demands made upon them by the large badly lit spaces in which they performed,[4] Liston preferred to give quiet and restrained performances.

Liston's attention to detail manifested itself in the concentration or "earnestness" with which he performed:

> The great merit of Liston – wrote the *New York Mirror* – is his earnestness. Kean does not appear more earnest than Liston at the loss of a pocket handkerchief, or being over-changed a shilling in a tavern bill. His whole soul seems to be absorbed in an affair of this kind. He does not bustle about or put himself in a passion in order to make the audience laugh at the ridiculous nature of the circumstances, as other actors do; but all the faculties of the man's mind seem concentrated to endeavour to convince or persuade, as the case may require, solely to save the said shilling, or regain the said handkerchief; and it is the contrast between the disproportion of the exertion employed and the importance of the object to be obtained ... that is so supremely ludicrous. ... It is a shrewd satire upon humanity, turning into burlesque the lofty pretensions – the power and knowledge and wit and wisdom of mankind, and presents a *stronger* and truer picture of the littleness of man and his pursuits than a thousand homilies.[5]

Such roles as Lubin Log, Tristram Sappy and Paul Pry gave particular scope for this sort of performance, in which human beings were seen at their most petty and their most stupid.

The earnestness and detail with which Liston invested his parts can be seen particularly in his performance of Sam Savory, a cook, in Joseph Lunn's *Fish out of Water*, first performed at the Haymarket in 1823. Savory is mistaken as the applicant for the post of secretary in the house of a gentleman who is looking for both a cook and a secretary. The applicant for the secretary's post, in the meantime, is mistaken for the would-be cook. This piece, which was later revived at the Olympic under the title of *The Cook and the Secretary*, enabled Liston to create a closely observed portrait of the unfortunate cook:

> The pompous consequence with which he carried out his culinary examination – the fidgety air with which he attended to the concoction of the chocolate – the consternation which agitated him during his interviews with *Sir George* – and, above all, his confusion, dismay and

vulgar submission, when obliged to write the penitential letter, were all in his very best style.[6]

The "culinary examination", in which Liston, as secretary, had to examine the supposed new candidate for cook, proved very amusing:

> there was the vanity of the culinary scholar, and the confident, questioning stare of quibbling experience ... (an actual cook) could not be more professionally important, more cool, collected, closed up in opinion made "confirmation strong" by ancient practice, in the examination of his Galenic candidate, than was Liston in his sententious enquiry of "how to make a dish of pheasants *à la braise?*" His visage relaxing into an acquiescent *hauteur* at the answer of his scholar – "with ham" – raised the spirit of laughter through the whole house. It was not contortion, it was *mind*, and showed the principle of self-valuation is the same in the first man of the kitchen as in the first of a Senate.[7]

The other particularly amusing moment was Liston's writing a letter confessing the mistake:

> Only imagine Liston, as the cook, directed to endite a penitent letter – all the gradations of his awkwardness and dismay – the rich blunders in orthography – the vain attempts to escape – the utter amazement of the long words which he cannot remember – the overtoppling misery – till he is happily dismissed to the kitchen![8]

Some of the "business" with which Liston's characters were provided was, of course, more traditional. Even so, it still helped to underline the "humours" of these characters and provided fuller opportunities for Liston to display his comic powers of observation. Food, for instance, was often used for comic effect. As Neddy Bray in *XYZ* he conveyed his confusion and embarrassment by continually stuffing buns into his mouth, whilst trying to talk at the same time. As Tristram Sappy his peevish selfishness came to the fore when the supposedly deaf Templeton continually helped himself to the food placed on Sappy's plate, before Sappy even had time to taste it. As Sir Hippington Miff in *Comfortable Lodgings* his fearful cowardice became apparent when he has to eat a meal which he suspected was poisoned. As Mr. Sedley in *A Gentleman in Difficulties* he waited on table, but could hardly restrain himself from partaking of the food and drink. His cowardice as Sir Andrew Aguecheek was demonstrated by a quick ascent of the proscenium arch, while as Van Dunder he displayed his stupidity by pretending to read a letter of which he could evidently not understand a single word. All his roles were enlivened by such business, although it was Liston's reaction to the circumstances rather than the circumstances themselves that provoked the audience's laughter.

Mistaken identity, as in *Fish Out of Water*, and disguise often place Liston's characters in situations that reveal their obduracy or cure their faults. In *Talk of the Devil* the intelligence of Dominique the Deserter is quickly grasped when he mistakes an intruder into his room for the Devil, a mistake which forms the pivot of the play. Lubin Log is tricked out of an arranged marriage, when he is duped by an actress disguised as a Princess. Sappy is fooled by Templeton's impersonation of a deaf man. Liston's characters are not only outwitted through the use of disguise; Long Singleton in *My Eleventh Day*, for instance, is cured of his jealousy as a result of the various disguises assumed by his young wife. Sometimes a Liston character is himself mistaken for someone else; the shaven-headed Gervase Skinner, whom Liston played during his first Olympic season, is mistaken for a lunatic and treated accordingly. Bowbell is assumed to be an "illustrious" personage and so a vulgar cockney marries a Princess. Such events are, of course, the norm of situation comedy and of farce, but Liston's reaction to these events provided an added source of humour.

Liston's reactions to events, be they good or bad, were all the more remarkable on account of his facial expression. As Bowbell, in cap and gown, he marched forlornly across the stage to his own funeral procession – suddenly, he stopped and looked despairingly at the audience. It was this acknowledgement of his audience, whilst remaining solemnly in character, that many found irresistible. Sometimes, it could be almost moving, as when in *Sweethearts and Wives*, he turned "that extremely full and plaintive moon of his visage – sad yet of a harvest-hue"[9] – towards the audience. Often, when playing some deadpan character, he would provoke laughter by his "side-bursting cock of the eye", although he was condemned for too frequently trusting to this device.[10] As Mawworm, recalled George Daniel, "he gathered up his face into a variety of farcical festoons and with a look in which inevitable stupidity and ludicrous surprise were oddly blended, seemed to wonder what in the world folks could see *in him* to laugh at!"[11] In thought Liston's face was especially comic – as Tristram Sappy:

> He squeezes up his lip between his forefinger and his thumb and casts his eye upwards with such a reflective comicality that it is impossible to refrain from loud laughter at the ludicrous inanity of the whole aspect.[12]

Occasionally, if he had to smile, the twist of his nose and mouth was another cause for laughter.

Liston's face was physically extraordinary, a characteristic due to nature rather than to exaggeration or grimace. "There is one face of Farley", wrote Charles Lamb, "one face of Knight, one (but what a one it is!) of Liston".[13] Once described as "a large mass of inanimate flesh",[14] his face nevertheless contained many interesting features. His "carp-like mouth", with its "ideotic hang of the underlip", contained "a most peculiar power of expression".[15] Leigh Hunt describes how his mouth and chin with the throat under it, "hung like an old bag".[16] His nose, which was considered insignificant both as to size and shape, featured dilated nostrils, which created rather a snub-nosed effect. His grey, "goggle" eyes, dull and lack-lustre in repose, could range in expression from stupidity to astonishment and even waken into occasional liveliness. In singular contrast his forehead was as fine as possible: "there is a speculation, a look out and elevation of character in it, as unlike the Liston of the stage as Lear is to King Pippin",[17] wrote Leigh Hunt. On closer inspection, Hazlitt observed that "part of the rich humour of Mr. Liston's face rises from his having lost a tooth in the front".[18] Leigh Hunt believed that audiences loved to "doat" on Liston's "oily, mantling face".[19]

Liston was particularly adept at emptying his face of both intelligence and expression:

> In his portraits of some of the heroes of cockney-land, he manages to exclude the slightest glimmering of intelligence from his countenance, and at the same time contrives to throw into it an air of conceit and self-satisfaction, which conveys to you that he is not only without an idea, but that any attempt to innoculate him with one would be altogether hopeless.[20]

Yet, however stupid, solemn or "deadpan" Liston looked, he managed to keep his audiences amused. Westland Marston recalled how:

> in almost every character he evinced quiet, intense self-satisfaction and ludicrous gravity in absurd sayings and doings. His humour was often to seem insensible to the ludicrous, and a look of utter unconsciousness on his serene and elongated face would accompany the utterance of some absurdity or sly jest, and rouse shouts of laughter, while he stood monumentally calm.[21]

Leigh Hunt wasn't so sure about the unconsciousness: "Liston was renowned", he said, "for an exquisitely ridiculous face and manner, rich with half-conscious, half-unconscious absurdity".[22] He may have been deadpan, but he somehow contrived to reveal to the audience that he knew what he was about.

Often, when Liston appeared on stage, his fellow-actors were so amused by his countenance that they could not keep a straight face. This happened not only in the London theatres, but also in the provinces. Once, when Liston played at Brighton, little Phyllis Glover was obliged to turn aside her face continually and other actors were in the same predicament, "while the cause of all this mirth stood with apparently unconscious gravity, leering and looking as man never looked before".[23] "So irresistably comic is the face of this gentleman", remarked the *Theatrical Investigator*, when Liston played Mug in Liverpool, "that the laughing mania extended itself from the audience to the stage, even before he uttered a sentence of his author".[24] So remarkable was the power of Liston' face, that many comedies and farces lost half their humour without it. "The jest is lost", claimed the *London Magazine*, "unless he prints his face or rather his whole person".[25]

Liston's face was his fortune. Yet, in contrast to his ludicrous appearance, he was blessed with an extremely well-proportioned body: 5ft 11 inches tall, he was considered, in his younger days, one of the finest-formed men in London.[26] As he grew older, he grew fatter, which increased in size another of his physical assets – a large, protuberant and pendulous posterior, which often added to his grotesque appearance on stage. He seems also to have been double-jointed – his looseness of hips and ability to relax his joints helped him particularly when he played ludicrous dancing parts and burlesqued the corps de ballet at the Kings Theatre. In his walk, the *Drama* considered, "there was something so excessively outré, that it has not infrequently thrown the whole theatre into convulsions of laughter".[27] His style of movement was implicit in the *London Magazine*'s description of how, at the Haymarket, he "flops about ... or goes waggling about the shallows of comedy".[28]

In foolish roles Liston could appear extremely awkward; in *Catch Him Who Can* "he dangled and swung about his arms and legs, as if they were upon wires".[29] His awkward movements were often accentuated by the slovenly, slouching posture he adopted. This is depicted in many prints, in which Liston invariably stands with shoulders hunched forward, knees slightly bent and hands in pockets. When he played affected or conceited roles, he tended to use exaggerated hand gestures, as can be seen in prints of Caper, Grizzle and Endless. In all, it seems that Liston was able to complement fatuity of expression with fatuity of movement. However, in more realistic characters, his posture could appear more relaxed; prints of Adam Brock, for instance, show Liston comfortably settled in an armchair, as if by his own fireside. He clearly modified movement and expression, according to the nature of the part he was playing.

This modification was also noticeable in his choice of costumes and wigs. Liston had a knack of dressing characters and selecting wigs to procure strong and memorable effects. The success of Lubin Log and of Paul Pry was partly due to this talent and in both Liston was praised for individualising them through the use of costume. Even if Liston looked absurd, it was for a purpose, to highlight character as much as for comic effect. Whether he wore the baggy Dutch bloomers of Van Dunder or the traditional costume of the broom girl, his face transmuted them into a portrait of absurdity. No wonder the *Times* commented that "his dress and appearance, of themselves alone, are sufficient commonly (as well as too much relied upon for that purpose) to carry through a piece".[30] The *Tatler* declared: "Liston is a finished artist – his dresses are the comicality of costume – his wigs work wonders".[31] Even so, although Liston wore exaggerated costumes in exaggerated parts, he did not depend on this sort of excess to raise laughter. Benson Earl Hill recalled how, in *Fish Out of Water*, Liston proved "that he did not depend on a grotesque appearance, at least on a queer dress".[32]

Liston's voice was as unique as his face. An early description in the *News* referred to Liston's "disadvantage of voice, which reminds us of the contented humdrum of a tabernacle preacher".[33] Marston describes Liston's voice as "oracular",[34] whilst the *New York Mirror* referred to "the deep sepulchral croak, in which he narrates petty grievances".[35] The *News* apart, most critics accepted his voice and the use he made of it. In *Catch Him Who Can* he "drawled out his sentences with a lisp and lackadaisical whine";[36] Hook referred to "the quaint exclamations and tremulous grumblings"[37] of Liston's voice. Hazlitt wrote that "his voice is rich with excellent conceit".[38] "Oh that benevolent fat voice!" exclaimed B. E. Hill.[39]

When it came to singing, Liston's voice proved rather inadequate when called upon to rival the singers at the King's Theatre, but he had no problem in singing comic songs or in burlesquing singers like Madame Catalani. He was adept at using accents, although in Scott adaptations his Scots accent was not always as precise as it might have been. He could manage the Yorkshire accent required for country parts adequately enough, but he was particularly skilled in cockney. Even so, Hazlitt found Liston's "marked cockneyism of pronouncing the V for the W" in Lubin Log "a hackneyed and cheap way of producing laughs".[40]

Liston's delivery can only be surmised, but his solemn delivery of his words seems to have been a source of humour. The seriousness of his expression, as he uttered one of his many catch-phrases – "Quite correct!", "Prodigious!", "Just dropped in! Hope I don't intrude!", "'Twould puzzle a Conjuror!" – probably provoked more laughter than his actual intonation. While Liston's manner of thus repeating a common observation drew laughter, he could also amuse through the emphasis he put on certain words. The *Brighton Gazette* drew attention to the scene in *The Young Quaker*, when Liston, as the servant Clod, desires Pink, a maid, to treat him with less *familiarity* or he will kick her downstairs. It found Liston's manner of pronouncing the word *familiarity* "inimitably droll", declaring that "there is something too excessively comic and peculiar in his voice, which it would be impossible to describe and which it would be vain to imitate".[41] In *XYZ*:

> one exclamation was alone, by the droll look which accompanied it, quite inimitable – "Did they ill-use you? Nasty Beasts!" We never witnessed a finer display of the comedian's power than in these two words; their effect was irresistable.[42]

Liston's manner and appearance on stage were so unique that it was difficult, at times, to separate the character from the actor. Admittedly, each character was differentiated, but Liston's idiosyncratic style contributed especially to his popularity in what, after all, was an age of "personality" actors. Marston suggests that he was able to adapt himself in some measure to various parts, including those of cockney, rustic and gentleman, but that his actual manner of playing all these different roles was rather similar.[43] He *Listonised* his parts, resolving them all, by a sort of alchemy, into something particularly his own. George Daniel noticed this tendency several times: as Ben, in *Love for Love*, Liston gave "a touch of all our old acquaintances – a running fire of Neddy Bray, Apollo Belvi, General Bombastes and Lord Grizzle";[44] when Liston played Governor Tempest in *The Wheel of Fortune*, the audience laughed heartily "not at the eccentricities of Governor Tempest, but at those of Mr. Liston".[45] *John Bull* considered that Paul Pry should have been called *John Liston*, "for John Liston, the inimitable and unique, makes all the plays which are attributed to other persons". (18/9/1825).

Even if Liston was recognisably himself in most of his parts, he was not monotonously so. "Liston is always the same", commented the *Mirror of the Stage*, "yet, like the chameleon, always varying from the effect of awakening accident".[46] His humour, however, had a lot to do with his highly personal style of performance:

> Liston brings every material home to his own workshop and places it, as it were, about his own person; he refers everything ludicrous to the

seriousness of his own delivery, the imperturbability of his features, and creates laughter by the evident unconsciousness that there can be anything to laugh at.[47]

According to the *Times* Liston had "the genuine quality which alone can make a great comedy actor: that of being comical in himself, without reference to the wit of the matter which he has to utter.[48]

Although the *Times* considered Liston a great comedy actor, others felt that he was merely a buffoon. George Daniel condemned Liston for frittering away his talents in "low buffooneries perpetrated by the lowest buffoons". As a result he "made a most lame and impotent conclusion, when he might have left a lasting impression".[49] Such a viewpoint is justified, if one considers that the actor serves the text; less so, if one accepts that the text can sometimes serve the actor. In some quarters *buffoon* was felt to be a most inappropriate term with which to describe Liston:

> ... (some) people think because Mr. Liston occasionally plays coarse and foolish parts in coarse and foolish farces, that Mr. Liston is, consequently, a coarse and foolish fellow, and only fit to amuse the uneducated vulgar; and as "grimace" and "buffoonery" are the two standing words used in abusing comedians, let their faults be what they may, they have not infrequently been applied to Liston. Now, if any one is free from what is meant by these two words, as set down in many dictionaries, it is this actor. The merits of his unparallelled countenance are passive, not active; and distortion would only render the countenance common-place, which in a state of blank repose is intensely ridiculous.[50]

In so far as Liston could be accused of buffoonery on stage, it was usually due to the fact that he could extract laughter from his audiences regardless of the part he was playing. Sometimes, though, he did resort to "gagging", the process of making fellow-actors laugh while on stage with him. Catherine Stephens seems to have been a frequent victim of such activities, a fact that annoyed Lord William Lennox, who wrote that Liston's "buffoonery was unworthy of an artist who held the position he did on the London boards".[51] Perhaps his audiences spoilt him and allowed him to get away with too much. He frequently improvised during performances, even conversed with the audience directly, and rarely played a new part for more than a few nights without adding extra dialogue.

A facility to improvise was probably quite helpful when so many new

parts had to be memorised in so short a space of time. On the first night of
Sweethearts and Wives, for instance, Liston was accused of sharing himself
with the audience and the prompter. As Old Rapid in *A Cure for the
Heartache*, "if he did not say what was exactly *set down* for him, he said
something quite as intellectual and infinitely more droll".[52] James
Boaden also noticed Liston's tendency to improvise, "when he enters to
soliloquize, or rather enjoy *himself* with the audience". "He could", said
Boaden, "deliver artful composition directly if he chose to do so; but either
for his author's sake, or his own, he is best, ad libitum, confined only by
the business of the play".[53] An instance of this tendency occurred one
new year's eve, when he was playing Mawworm in *The Hypocrite*. He was
interrupted by some noisy holiday-makers in the gallery, as he was
uttering:

Ignorant wretches! Ye'll all go the Devil!

Raising himself up with burlesque dignity and with much sternness eyeing
his interrupters, he exclaimed loudly:

Silence! Silence! I say, ye noisy, *whistling*, infatuated wretches! – ye will
all, all, go to the Devil! I whistle ye off!

Tremendous applause followed and even the performers laughed:

And ye laugh too, do ye? added Liston, looking round reprovingly at his
fellow-actors.[54]

Liston's ad-libbing, far from rendering him a mere buffoon, demonstrated the close relationship he was able to establish with his audience,
no mean achievement in the large auditorium of a patent theatre. He
would often draw laughter by fixing his eye on someone in the pit,
treatment that proved most effective when troublemakers were in the
audience. Sometimes he addressed members of the audience directly –
when someone called out "Bravo, Liston" after a performance of *Paul Pry*,
Liston replied, "Sir, you're very good". On another occasion he took the
audience by surprise by wishing them a very good night. He had, said
George Wightwick, "(as no other actors would have been allowed) a
private and confidential understanding with his audience".[55] This was
probably the result of technical skill rather than buffoonery, for, whatever
advantages Liston possessed in his own person, it was the skill with which
he used these advantages that enabled him to win over and control his
audiences.

Some of the accounts of Liston's artistry as an actor seem to contradict the accusations tht he was slovenly or just fooled about. Ben Webster, who had first hand experience of acting with Liston, wrote:

Indeed, the artist-like manner in which he gets up his characters must be seen to be credited. He scarcely ever produces an unstudied effect, either in word, look or gesture. It is his constant custom to attend the first two rehearsals of any new piece he is to act in, that the sides of the entrances may be duly arranged; he then goes diligently to work, and at the next rehearsal, which takes place four or five days after, comes perfect, and so on to the day of the performance; by which time he is so mellowed in the matter, that the words become a secondary consideration, and he is thus enabled to devote the whole force of his mind to the business of the scene.[56]

The *Illustrated London News* bears out Liston's careful approach:

Every character he sustained always bore the stamp of profound thought; he never did a thing in his profession without having first satisfied his mind why it should be done. His study was not (technically speaking) quick, but it was very certain; few actors could have given their authors more correctly.[57]

Both of these accounts, written at the end of Liston's life, probably refer in particular to performances in the disciplined environment of the Olympic Theatre. Madame Vestris recalled how she once overheard Liston cursing and spluttering as he stood at the side-scene waiting to go on in a scene of comic rage, which again suggests that Liston put a certain amount of effort into his performances. Yet even if Liston was not so painstaking with some of the mediocre roles assigned him earlier in his career, he always displayed certain skills as an actor. "He appears thoroughly to have studied the art of acting", stated the *Authentic Memoirs of the Green-room*, "and to have attained the most difficult of all its parts – forgetfulness of himself and a continual recollection of the character he assumes".[58] Perhaps he did not so much *forget* himself as through himself create the part he played: his "art" was creative:

Give Liston the *ghost* of a character, he invested its thinness in corporal substance; or, to choose another illustration, an outline or figure was all that was wanting to his art; he infused into it the richness of his own comic imagination, in aid of irresistable features, and completed the work designed by another hand.[59]

As a result he was able to give performances that seemed so natural that his artistry was concealed:

> Mr. Liston is certainly the most simple or natural actor on the stage; there is a sort of sincerity about his manner. It presents to your observation not the able and artful comedian, the semblance of the person represented; but he places you at once in the presence of the identical person himself.[60]

The word "natural" was often used to describe Liston's acting. Leigh Hunt considered that he could play characters who were true to nature or who might be considered "deviations" from nature with equal truth. When Liston first visited Edinburgh, the *Evening Courant* considered him not "a caricaturist, but a *natural* actor; the colouring given by him is perfectly true, but its beauties cannot be discovered by a glance".[61] The *Authentic Memoirs* praised Liston because he never deviated from Nature's path.[62] His Adam Brock, Monsieur Papelard, Mr. Gillman and many of his Olympic roles were praised because they appeared so "natural". Not everyone agreed that Liston's acting was natural. Mrs. Oxberry claimed that he could represent habits and peculiarities, but that he could not portray the heart and mind of a man. Natural, she considered, was too good a term for Liston; so did the *Drama*, which felt Liston failed to show a sufficiently just discrimination and development of human passion.[63] Yet the *Examiner* considered that, with Liston, "the nicest discrimination of feeling has always given an additional richness and truth to the broadest effects".[64]

Liston's most outstanding characteristic on stage was, perhaps, his repose. He appeared so relaxed that all he did seemed entirely effortless; this effortlessness probably defines more closely the secret of Liston's technique than can a vaguer, more open-ended term like "naturalness". "Other actors labour to be comic", wrote James Boaden. "I see nothing like labour or system in Liston".[65] Cole, the biographer of Charles Kean, felt Liston's "great and distinguishing excellence lay in the ease and apparent unconsciousness with which he convulsed an audience. There was no hard straining, no deep delving for a joke ..."[66] Liston never seemed to exert himself: "the ease of it is all its charm" wrote the *Theatrical Looker-on* of Liston's acting.[67] The secret of this seeming effortlessness lay, of course, in his face:

> Liston never oversteps his part by attempting to do too much. Endowed with an irresistably comic countenance, he has nothing to do but express the commonest observations in the simplest manner, and his

audience is delighted, because they think they see Nature, undisguised by effort.[68]

The effortlessness and restraint with which he performed frequently won him praise for being a "quiet" actor. *Blackwood's Magazine* considered him the best "quiet" comedian it could remember, for he made no obvious attempts to draw laughter from his audiences.[69]

Because of this ability to amuse and provoke laughter without apparent effort, a trait that distinguished him from many of his fellow-comedians, Liston was widely praised for his *originality* and "inimitable" became a favourite term by which to describe him. Allied to his technical skill as a comedian was the ability to create totally new characters and make them uniquely his own. Liston copied no-one and no-one was able to copy him, with the result that he stood alone in his own particular line and other actors played his special roles with only partial success. "His acting", claimed the *Drama*, "is of that peculiarly original nature as to defy anything like successful imitation or even competition".[70] Hazlitt considered Liston as an author rather than an actor: "he makes his parts out of his own head or face, in a sort of *brown study*, with very little reference".[71] Whenever Liston appeared in a new part, he usually revealed something fresh and unexpected – for his originality lay not only in his unique personal appearance and effortless technique, but also in his creative skills as an actor.

So unique and distinctive an actor as Liston evidently was might not be expected to harmonise with his fellow-actors. "I do not think his style mixes well", said Boaden; "he does not concur in any general effect – he is alone as well with others in the scene as when he enters to soliloquise. ..."[72] Hazlitt felt that Liston did not play so well to anyone else, as he did to himself.[73] Yet, in many productions, Liston was praised for the contribution he made to the ensemble playing: *Paul Pry, The Happiest Day of My Life* and *The Two Figaros* all provide evidence of this. He also worked well with actresses like Mrs. Glover and Mrs. Orger, often creating convincing pictures of marital discord or domestic bliss with them. His team-work with Charles Mathews the elder was well known. They formed "a pair of players who discourse too excellent a music together ever to be put properly asunder".[74] Liston worked extremely well with actors like the elder Mathews and William Farren, whose styles of acting and types of role complimented his own.

Even if critical accounts of Liston's acting are inevitably subjective and therefore sometimes contradictory, they make it clear that he possessed a formidable talent. In the parts he played, in the use he made of his own physical appearance, in his originality, repose and restraint, he offered something that no other comic actor was able to provide. Even the pathos, traditionally associated with great comedians, was present – some critics felt that they should have pitied, rather than laughed at, such grotesques as Lubin Log and Tristram Sappy. The public were fascinated by him, a compliment he repaid in the world of characters he created. He was the Dickens of the early nineteenth century stage, creating his own carefully observed, eccentric and highly comic world. Ludicrous in himself, he was able to make his characters ludicrous without exaggeration or effort. In the words of E. B. Watson:

To be himself was to be extravagant. He did not act low comedy – he was its embodiment.[75]

Appendix

The Roles of John Liston
A Selective List

During his thirty two years on the London stage Liston played over 400 roles, many of which were so ephemeral that they only lasted one night. Below are listed those roles which are referred to in the text or which were performed sufficiently to be worth recording. Original roles created by Liston are marked with an asterisk. The dates given for these roles and, as far as possible, for the other roles listed, are for Liston's first London performance. (It is worth noting that a further 200 roles were played by Liston in the provinces between 1799–1805 and that Newcastle Public Library holds an almost complete set of Newcastle playbills for the years during which Liston belonged to the Newcastle company.)

Date	Role	Play	Theatre
10/ 6/1805	Sheepface	*The Village Lawyer* (W. Macready)	HM
14/ 6/1805	Zekiel Homespun	*The Heir at Law* (G. Colman)	HM
18/ 6 /1805	John Lump	*The Review* (G. Colman)	HM
19/ 6/1805	Dan	*John Bull* (G. Colman)	HM
24/ 6/1805	Robin Roughead	*Fortune's Frolic* (J. T. Allingham)	HM
8/ 8/1805	Motley	*The Castle Spectre* (M. G. Lewis)	HM
19/ 8/1805	Frank	*Three and a Deuce* (P. Hoare)	HM
15/10/1805	Jacob Gawkey	*The Chapter of Accidents* (S. Lee)	CG
		(Covent Garden debut; performed HM 5/7/1805)	

Date	Role	Play	Theatre
16/10/1805	Solomon	*The Quaker* (I. Jackman)	CG
18/10/1805	*Memmo	*Rugantino* (M. G. Lewis)	CG
8/11/1805	Sim	*Wild Oats* (J. O'Keeffe)	CG
14/11/1805	*Nicholas	*The Delinquent* (F. Reynolds)	CG
28/11/1805	Diggory	*All the World's a Stage* (I. Jackman)	CG
30/11/1805	Master Stephen	*Everyman in his Humour* (B. Jonson)	CG
28/1/1806	*Gaby Grim	*We Fly by Night* (G. Colman)	CG
7/2/1806	Slender	*The Merry Wives of Windsor* (Shakespeare)	CG
27/3/1806	Governor Tempest	*The Wheel of Fortune* (R. Cumberland)	CG
1/4/1806	Arthur	*The White Plume* (T. Morton)	CG
13/5/1806	Shenkin	*Folly as it Flies* (F. Reynolds)	CG
14/5/1806	Lord Grizzle	*Tom Thumb* (Fielding adapted O'Hara) (First performed at HM 21/6/1806)	CG
12/6/1806	*Jeffrio de Pedrillos	*Catch Him Who Can* (T. Hook)	HM
9/7/1806	*Flourish	*Five Miles Off* (T. Dibdin)	HM
22/7/1806	Jeffrey	*Animal Magnetism* (E. Inchbald)	HM
15/11/1806	*Michael	*Adrian and Orilla* (W. Dimond)	CG
20/11/1806	*Don Utopio	*The Deserts of Arabia* (F. Reynolds)	CG
11/12/1806	*Chequer	*Arbitration* (F. Reynolds)	CG
7/3/1807	Polonius	*Hamlet* (Shakespeare)	CG
16/7/1807	*Phillip	*The Fortress* (T. Hook)	HM
6/8/1807	Don Whiskerandos	*The Critic* (R. B. Sheridan)	HM
27/8/1807	*Matthew Method	*Music Mad* (T. Hook)	HM
17/11/1807	*Hector	*Two Faces under a Hood* (T. Dibdin)	CG
1/12/1807	*Molino	*The Blind Boy* (J. Kenney)	CG
25/2/1808	*Caper	*Who Wins* (J. T. Allingham)	CG
21/4/1808	Thurio	*The Two Gentlemen of Verona* (Shakespeare)	CG
21/6/1808	*Pedrillo	*Plot and Counterplot or The Portrait of Cervantes* (C. Kemble) (staged at HM 30/6/1808)	CG
29/7/1808	*Henry Augustus Mug	*The Africans* (G. Colman)	HM

Date	Role	Play	Theatre
31/8/1808	*Obadiah Broadbrim	Yes or No (I. Pocock)	HM
10/11/1808	*Baron Altradoff	The Exile (F. Reynolds)	CG
17/5/1809	Octavian	The Mountaineers (G. Colman)	CG
17/6/1809	Scrub	The Beaux Strategem (Farquhar)	HM
1/7/1809	*Apollo Belvi	Killing no Murder (T. Hook)	HM
4/7/1809	Timothy Quaint	The Soldier's Daughter (A. Cherry)	HM
10/7/1809	*L'Eclair	The Foundling of the Forest (W. Dimond)	HM
12/8/1809	Duke's Servant	High Life Below Stairs (J. Townley)	HM
16/8/1809	Launcelot Gobbo	The Merchant of Venice (Shakespeare)	HM
21/8/1809	Bob Acres	The Rivals (R. B. Sheridan)	HM
23/8/1809	Clod	The Young Quaker (J. O'Keeffe)	HM
7/8/1810	*Bombastes Furioso	Bombastes Furioso (W. B. Rhodes)	HM
11/12/1810	*Neddy Bray	XYZ (G. Colman)	CG
5/1/1811	Malvolio	Twelfth Night (Shakespeare)	CG
5/2/1811	*Macloon	The Knight of Snowdoun (T. Morton)	CG
26/7/1811	*Rogero	The Quadrupeds of Quedlinbergh (G. Colman)	HM
7/8/1811	Tony Lumpkin	She Stoops to Conquer (Goldsmith)	HM
		(Performed for Drury Lane Debut 28/1/1823)	
10/8/1811	Sir Benjamin Backbite	The School for Scandal (R. B. Sheridan)	HM
27/8/1811	Squire Richard	The Provoked Husband (Cibber & Vanbrugh)	HM
18/12/1811	Shelty	The Highland Reel (J. O'Keeffe)	CG
31/1/1812	*Diego	The Virgin of the Sun (F. Reynolds)	CG
24/4/1812	*Dimdim	The Secret Mine (T. Dibdin)	CG
16/6/1812	Romeo	Romeo and Juliet (Shakespeare)	CG
17/9/1812	Midas	Midas (K. O'Hara)	CG
6/10/1812	*Benmoussaff	The Aethiop (W. Dimond)	CG
24/10/1812	Moll Flaggon	The Lord of the Manor (J. Burgoyne)	CG
20/11/1812	*Lubin Log	Love, Law and Physic (J. Kenney)	CG
2/12/1812	*Jacquez	The Renegade (F. Reynolds, based on Dryden's Don Sebastian)	CG

Date	Role	Play	Theatre
25/ 2/1813	*Captain Dash	At Home (Sir H. B. Dudley, ascribed)	CG
27/ 4/1813	*Suckling	Education (T. Morton)	CG
17/ 6/1813	*Ophelia	Hamlet Travestie (J. Poole)	CG
19/ 8/1813	Monsieur de Paris	The Waltz (S. J. Arnold) (adapted from Wycherley, The Gentleman Dancing Master)	LYC
21/10/1813	*Karl	The Miller and his Men (I. Pocock)	CG
1/ 2/1814	'Peter	The Farmer's Wife (C. Dibdin)	CG
20/ 4/1814	*Gosling	Debtor and Creditor (J. Kenney)	CG
15/ 6/1814	Solomon Grundy	Who Wants a Guinea (G. Colman)	CG
16/ 8/1814	*Mr Liston (Harlequin)	Harlequin Hoax (T. Dibdin)	LYC
30/ 9/1814	*Blaise	The Forest of Bondi (J. Kenney)	CG
12/11/1814	*Pedrigo Potts	John of Paris (I. Pocock)	CG
27/ 3/1815	*Buffardo	Zembucca (I. Pocock)	CG
15/ 9/1815	*Martin	The Magpie, or the Maid (I. Pocock)	CG
25/10/1815	*Mimiski	John du Bart (I. Pocock)	CG
20/11/1815	Justice Dorus	Cymon (D. Garrick)	CG
17/ 1/1816	Bottom	A Midsummer Night's Dream (Shakespeare adapted F. Reynolds)	
8/ 2/1816	Pompey	Measure for Measure (Shakespeare)	CG
12/ 3/1816	*Dominie Sampson	Guy Mannering (D. Terry)	CG
12/11/1816	*Fogrun	The Slave (T. Morton)	CG
18/ 1/1817	Humorous Lieutenant	The Humorous Lieutenant (Beaumont & Fletcher, adapted F. Reynolds)	
20/ 5/1817	Leporello	The Libertine (I. Pocock) (based on Don Giovanni)	CG
29/ 5/1817	Cloten	Cymbeline (Shakespeare)	CG
21/ 2/1818	*Pequillo	Zuma (T. Dibdin)	CG
12/ 3/1818	*Baillie Jarvie	Rob Roy (I. Pocock)	CG
30/ 3/1818	*Josselin	Marquis de Carabas (unknown)	CG
13/ 4/1818	*Fitzcloddy	Who's my Father (T. Morton)	CG
6/ 5/1818	*Werther	The Sorrows of Werther (J. Lunn)	CG

Date	Role	Play	Theatre
12/6/1818	Old Rapid	A Cure for the Heartache (T. Morton)	CG
17/7/1818	Lingo	The Agreeable Surprise (J. O'Keeffe)	HM
11/8/1818	*Fuddle	Nine Points of the Law (R. Jameson)	HM
13/10/1818	Figaro	The Barber of Seville (D. Terry)	CG
6/3/1819	Figaro	The Marriage of Figaro (H. Bishop)	CG
17/4/1819	*Dumbiedikes	The Heart of Mid-Lothian (D. Terry)	CG
20/7/1819	*Sir Onesiphorus Puddefoot Bart.	Wet Weather (T. Hook)	HM
14/8/1819	Lord Duberly	The Heir at Law (G. Colman) (2nd London appearance in role)	HM
28/8/1819	*Sir Peter Pigwiggin	Pigeons and Crows (T. Moncrieff)	HM
11/12/1819	Dromio of Syracuse	The Comedy of Errors (Shakespeare adapted F. Reynolds)	CG
25/1/1820	*Jonathan Oldbuck	The Antiquary (D. Terry adapted I. Pocock's 1818 version)	CG
2/3/1820	*Wamba	Ivanhoe (S. Beazley)	CG
22/2/1820	*Nicholas Twill	Too Late for Dinner (R. Jones)	CG
22/4/1820	*Jocrisse	Henri Quatre (T. Morton)	CG
12/8/1820	*Sam Swipes	Exchange no Robbery (T. Hook)	HM
31/8/1820	*Barnaby Buz	Dog Days in Bond Street (W. Dimond)	HM
8/11/1820	Sir Andrew Aguecheek	Twelfth Night (Shakespeare adapted F. Reynolds)	CG
20/2/1821	Fratioso	Don John or The Two Violettas (F. Reynolds' version of Buckingham's adaptation of Beaumont & Fletcher's The Chances)	CG
29/11/1821	Launce	The Two Gentlemen of Verona (Shakespeare adapted F. Reynolds)	CG
14/2/1822	*Dalgetty	Montrose (I. Pocock)	CG
11/5/1822	*Pengoose	The Law of Java (G. Colman)	CG
31/5/1822	Sir Bashful Constant	The Way to Keep Him (A. Murphy)	CG
11/7/1822	*Peter Finn	Peter Finn (R. Jones)	HM
26/7/1822	Peeping Tom	Peeping Tom of Coventry (J. O'Keeffe)	HM

Date	Role	Play	Theatre
26/8/1822	*Delph	Family Jars (J. Lunn)	HM
9/9/1822	*Lord Scribbleton	Morning, Noon and Night (T. Dibdin)	HM
15/2/1823	*Tristram Sappy	Deaf as a Post (J. Poole)	DL
18/6/1823	*Mr Smith	Mrs Smith (J. H. Payne)	HM
7/7/1823	*Billy Lackaday	Sweethearts and Wives (J. Kenney)	HM
26/8/1823	*Sam Savory	Fish out of Water (J. Lunn)	HM
1/12/1823	Mawworm	The Hypocrite (I. Bickerstaffe) (Royal Command performance: first performed HM 13/8/1822 DL 7/5/1823)	DL
13/1/1824	*Philander	Philandering (S. Beazley)	DL
1/5/1824	Lucio	Measure for Measure (Shakespeare)	DL
10/8/1824	*Pedrosa	Alcaid (J. Kenney)	HM
11/9/1824	*Van Dunder	'Twould Puzzle a Conjuror (J. Poole)	HM
29/7/1825	*Grojan	Quite Correct (C. Boaden)	HM
24/8/1825	*Sir Hilary Heartease	Roses and Thorns (J. Lunn)	HM
13/9/1825	*Paul Pry	Paul Pry (J. Poole)	HM
12/6/1826	*Simon Pengander	'Twixt the Cup and the Lip (J. Poole)	HM
28/7/1826	*Knipper Clipper	Thirteen to the Dozen (J. Kenney)	HM
14/8/1826	*Oliver Frumpton	Poor Relations (unknown)	HM
6/11/1826	*Pong Wong	Pong Wong (Charles Mathews the younger) (Duet with Madame Vestris)	HM
	Broom Girl		HM
1/3/1827	*Antonio	The Trial of Love (G. Soane)	DL
10/3/1827	*Sir Hippington Miff	Comfortable Lodgings (R. B. Peake)	DL
4/10/1827	*Bowbell	The Illustrious Stranger (J. Kenney)	DL
31/1/1828	*Tom Tadpole	The Haunted Inn (R. B. Peake)	DL
1/3/1828	Corporal Foss	The Poor Gentleman (G. Colman)	DL
17/4/1828	Ben	Love for Love (Congreve)	DL
27/5/1828	*Felix Mudberry	Ups and Downs (J. Poole)	DL
11/12/1828	*Adam Brock	Charles XII (J. R. Planché)	DL
12/2/1829	*Paul Shack	Master's Rival (R. B. Peake)	DL
21/2/1829	*Jasper Addlewitz	Peter the Great (J. Kenney)	DL
21/5/1829	*Monsieur Papelard	Partizans (J. R. Planché)	DL

Date	Role	Play	Theatre
29/7/1829	*Mr Gillman	The Happiest Day of my Life (J. B. Buckstone)	HM
26/8/1829	Mr Cool	All's Right (J. R. Planché) (Repeated Olympic 21/1/1833)	HM
31/8/1829	Baron Wildenheim	Lovers' Vows (E. Inchbald)	HM
3/11/1829	Mr Janus	Snakes in the Grass (J. B. Buckstone)	DL
4/2/1830	*Achille Bonbon	The National Guard (J. R. Planché)	DL
11/11/1830	*Jack Humphries	Turning the Tables (J. Poole)	DL
19/3/1831	*Narcissus Stubble	Highways and Byways (B. N. Webster)	DL
16/4/1831	*Pierre Galliard	Legion of Honour (J. R. Planché)	DL
1/10/1831	*Dominique	Talk of the Devil (S. Beazley)	OLYM
10/10/1831	*Placid	I'll be your Second (G. H. B. Rodwell)	OLYM
24/10/183	*Gervase Skinner	Gervase Skinner (unknown)	OLYM
21/11/1831	*Augustus Galopade	The Widow (J. T. Allingham) (revised version of Who Wins)	OLYM
16/1/1832	*Price Prettyman	He's Not A-miss (C. Dance)	OLYM
28/2/1832	*Long Singleton	My Eleventh Day (T. H. Bayly)	OLYM
15/3/1832	*Von Noodle	The Young Hopefuls (J. Poole)	OLYM
1/10/1832	*Fluid	The Water Party (C. Dance)	OLYm
29/10/1832	*Mr Brown	Kill or Cure (C. Dance)	OLYM
4/2/1833	*Tim Tartlet	The Cook and the Secretary (J. Lunn) (revised version of Fish out of Water)	OLYM
30/9/1833	*Septimus Lovebond	Look at Home (C. Dance)	OLYM
28/10/1833	*Mortimer Mims	Paired Off (J. Parry)	OLYM
28/11/1833	*Jasper Touchwood	Hush Money (G. Dance)	OLYM
9/12/1833	*Mr Flinch	Fighting by Proxy (J. Kenney)	OLYM
16/1/1834	*Baron Dunderhoof	Dancing for Life (J. Kenney)	OLYM
24/5/1834	*Oliver Sanguine	Pleasant Dreams (C. Dance)	CG
29/9/1834	*Pequillo	My Friend the Governor (J. R. Planché)	OLYM
23/10/1834	*Icarus Hawk	The Retort Courteous (unknown)	OLYM

10/11/1834	*Lucius Lot	Name the Winner (J. G. Millingen)	OLYM
27/11/1834	*Edward Dulcimer	How To Get Off (C. Dance)	OLYM
5/ 1/1835	*Peter Buzzard	A Scene of Confusion (unknown)	OLYM
26/ 1/1835	*Tricolore	Not a Word (J. Kenney)	OLYM
23/ 2/1835	*Mr Paradise	Hearts and Diamonds (D. W. Jerrold)	OLYM
12/ 3/1835	*Major Limkey	An Affair of Honour (W. Leman Rede)	OLYM
28/ 9/1835	*Mr Sedley	A Gentleman in Difficulties (T. H. Bayly)	OLYM
8/10/1835	*Magnus Lobb	The Two Queens (J. B. Buckstone)	OLYM
26/10/1835	*Becafico	The Man's an Ass (D. W. Jerrold)	OLYM
16/11/1835	*Mr Dibbs	The Beau Ideal (S. Lover)	OLYM
7/12/1835	*Tim Topple	The Old and Young Stager (W. Leman Rede)	OLYM
21/12/1835	*Maximum Hogflesh	Barbers at Court (E. Mayhew & G. Smith)	OLYM
1/ 3/1836	*Mr Lillywhite	Forty and Fifty (T. H. Bayly)	OLYM
20/10/1836	*Christopher Strap	A Pleasant Neighbour (E. Planché)	OLYM
30/11/1836	*Figaro	The Two Figaros (J. R. Planché)	OLYM
3/ 5/1837	*Monsieur Champignon	A Peculiar Position (J. R. Planché)	OLYM

ABBREVIATIONS

HM – *Theatre Royal, Haymarket*   DL – *Theatre Royal, Drury Lane*
CG – *Theatre Royal, Covent Garden*   OLYM – *Olympic Theatre*
LYC – *English Opera House, Lyceum*

Notes

Chapter 1

1 W. Oxberry, *Oxberry's Dramatic Mirror* (London, 1828), p. 331. The Oxberry memoir of Liston is very unsympathetic and needs to be considered with caution, even though it contains one of the fullest accounts of Liston's life available. Webster, in his Introduction to J. R. Planché's *The Two Figaros* in the *Acting National Drama*, I, (London, 1837) provides a more favourable account. The other most useful account of Liston's life is contained in the obituary printed in the *Illustrated London News*, VIII (28 March, 1846), 213. An unidentified clipping, undated, among the Liston Clippings in the Harvard Theatre Collection provides information about Liston's father in an account written by someone who claims to have been taught by Liston when he was employed as a schoolmaster. Although the date of Liston's birth is disputed, his death certificate states that he was 70 when he died in 1846, which makes 1776 the most likely date of birth.

2 W. Barrow, *An Essay on Education* (London, 1804), II, 285.

3 Two accounts of the incident described here exist: G. Raymond, *Memoirs of Robert William Elliston, Comedian* (London, 1846), II, pp. 106–109 and A. L. Nelson & B. Gilbert Cross (eds.), *Drury Lane Journal: Selections from James Winston's Diaries 1819–27* (London, 1974), p. 134. This is Winston's entry for 23/8/1826: he is recording an anecdote told him by the playwright Macfarren, who had been a pupil of Liston's at the time. Raymond's account, although it differs in certain details, was probably gleaned from Winston. Another ex-pupil (see: unidentified clipping, undated, Liston Clippings, Harvard Theatre Collection) draws attention to the ill-feeling between Liston and Pownall and describes the fracas that led to Liston's dismissal.

4 C. B. Hogan (ed.), *The London Stage, 1660–1800. Part 5: 1776–1800* (Southern Illinois, 1968), III, 2196. Hogan refers to Liston's name among the list of new performers for the Haymarket's 1799 season, now in the Harvard Theatre Collection.

5 Dublin Playbills, Harvard Theatre Collection.

6 Unidentified clipping, undated, Theatre Museum.

7 A. Mathews, *Tea-Table Talk* (London, 1844), II, pp. 290–312. As a close family friend of Liston Ann Mathews' account, if slightly embellished, is likely to have come from Liston himself. Although no Durham playbills for 1801 survive, the *Newcastle Advertiser*, 27 June & 4 July, 1801, reports that Mrs Siddons is appearing at Durham.

8 A. Mathews, *Op. cit.*

9 *Ibid.*

10 *Ibid.* See also: *Illustrated London News*, VIII (28 March, 1846), 213.

11 *Monthly Mirror*, XV (March, 1803), 206–207.

12 Oxberry, p. 333.

13 *Ibid.*

14 A. Mathews, *Memoirs of Charles Mathews, Comedian* (London, 1838–39), I, 358–360 & 412.

15 F. Kemble, *Records of a Girlhood* (New York, 1879), I, 37.

16 *Dramatic Magazine*, June, 1830.

Chapter 2

1 B. N. Webster, *Acting National Drama*, I, Introduction to J. R. Planché, *The Two Figaros*, p. 6.
2 *Morning Chronicle*, 16 October, 1805.
3 Webster, I, 6.
4 Liston wrote to De Wilde for a "character portrait" of Jacob Gawkey, after the editor of the *Monthly Mirror* had requested a portrait of that character for publication. See: Manuscript Letter, dated 29 October, Garrick Club Library. The other three De Wilde portraits of Liston now hang in the Garrick Club.
5 This was particularly the case with Mathews. See: Mathews, *Memoirs of Charles Mathews, Comedian*, I, 421.
6 R. H. Barham, *Life and Remains of T. E. Hook* (London, 1853), p. 12.
7 *Ibid.*, p. 13.
8 Clipping, undated, from *The Lady's Monthly Museum*, Princeton University Library.
9 Drury Lane Playbills, British Library.
10 *Theatrical Observer*, 8 January, 1828. Just before a banking scandal broke, Mrs Liston persuaded her husband to withdraw £8,000 he had invested with the bank in question.
11 Oxberry, p. 337.
12 Unidentified clipping, undated. *Dramatic Memoirs and Criticisms of Eminent Performers* in Dramatic Biography Theatre Cuttings, II, British Library.
13 Webster, I, 8.
14 G. Daniel, Introduction to K. O'Hara, *Tom Thumb, Cumberlands British Theatre* (London, 1829). XXIII.
15 P. P. Howe (ed.), *W. Hazlitt: Complete Works* (London, 1930), VI, 159.
16 *News*, 28 July, 1805.
17 Richard Ryan, *Dramatic Table Talk* (London, 1825), I, pp. 218–219.
18 *Authentic Memoirs of the Green-Room* (London, 1814?), p. 105.
19 *Monthly Mirror*, N.S.II (March, 1808), 266.
20 Hazlitt, VI, 159.
21 Oxberry, p. 334.
22 *Op. cit.*, p. 98.
23 *Ibid.*, p. 99.
24 *Dramatic Memoirs and Criticisms* (London, 1808), p. 3.

Chapter 3

1 *Statesman*, 23 October, 1809.
2 W. MacQueen-Pope, *Haymarket, Theatre of Perfection* (London, 1948), p. 211.
3 Manuscript Letter, dated 29 June, 1811, Theatre Museum.
4 *Theatrical Looker-On* (Birmingham), I (14 November, 1822), 97.
5 See: R. C. Leslie, *Autobiographical Recollections* (London, 1860), I, pp. 252–253 and J. R. Planché, *Recollections and Reflections* (London, 1872), I, 125–126.
6 Hazlitt, V, 192.
7 *Ibid.*, XII, 67–68.
8 G. Daniel, Introduction to J. Kenne, *Love, Law and Physic, Cumberland's British Theatre* (London, 1829), XXIV.
9 *Drama*, January, 1824.
10 *London Magazine*, V (July, 1822), 186. A picture by G. Clint, depicting the second act of the play, now hangs in the Garrick Club.
11 *New York Mirror*, 5 March, 1831.
12 *Ibid.*
13 *Drama*, January, 1824.
14 *Ibid.*
15 Hazlitt, V, 193.
16 W. C. Oulton, *A History of the Theatres of London* (London, 1818), III, 186.
17 Hazlitt, XVIII, 197.
18 L. E. Holman, *Lamb's "Barbara S-"* (London, 1935), p. 70.

19 Edwin. W. Marrs Jnr. (ed.), *The Letters of Charles and Mary Anne Lamb* (Ithaca and London, 1978), III, Letter dated 30 March, 1810.
20 Mathews, *Memoirs of Charles Mathews, Comedian*, II, pp. 64–65.
21 *Ibid.*, p. 167.
22 *Ibid.*, p. 348.
23 *Authentic Memoirs of the Green-Room* (London, 1814?), pp. 103–106.
24 *Examiner*, 29 January, 1815.
25 Hazlitt, XVIII, 218.
26 *Ibid.*, V, 273.

Chapter 4

1 Hazlitt, V, 275.
2 *Quarterly Review*, XVII (April, 1817), 155. The context in which this remark occurs is a critical attack on Hazlitt's pretensions to rival Addison and Steele.
3 *Examiner*, 26 December, 1819, quoted in L. H. and C. W. Houtchens (eds.), *Leigh Hunt's Dramatic Criticism* (New York, 1949), p. 328.
4 F. Reynolds, *The Life and Times of Frederick Reynolds* (London, 1826), II, 408.
5 Eluned Brown (ed.), *The London Theâtre 1811–1866, Selections from the Diary of Henry Crabb Robinson* (London, 1966), p. 33.
6 Quoted in A. C. Sprague, *Shakespeare and the Actors* (Cambridge Mass., 1943), p. 6.
7 *Examiner*, 12 November, 1820.
8 *Theatrical Observer*, 4 December, 1821.
9 *Ibid.*, 25 May, 1822.
10 Hazlitt, V, 283.
11 *Ibid.*, V, 292.
12 *Ibid.*, VXIII, 291.
13 H. Grierson (ed.), *The Letters of Sir Walter Scott – 1815–1817* (London, 1932–37), IV, 438.
14 G. Daniel, Introduction to D. Terry, *Guy Mannering, Cumberland's British Theatre* (London, 1829), XLIII.
15 Lord William Pitt Lennox, *Celebrities I have Known* (London, 1876), I, 262.
16 *Theatrical Observer*, 4 October, 1821.
17 H. A. White, *Sir Walter Scott's Novels on the Stage* in Albert S. Cook (ed.), *Yale Studies in English*, LXXVI (Yale University Press, 1927), p. 63. White is quoting Lockhart.
18 *London Magazine* V (March, 1822), 293.
19 *Op. cit.*, XIV (March, 1819), 229.
20 Oxberry, 336.
21 Inscribed on the back of a playbill, in the author's collection, advertising this performance.
22 *Theatrical Inquisitor*, IX (October, 1816), 264.
23 J. Genest, *Some Account of the English Stage* (Bath, 1832), VIII, 262.
24 Mathews, *Memoirs of Charles Mathews, Comedian*, II, 403.
25 T. S. Munden, *Memoirs of Joseph Shepherd Munden, Comedian*, (London, 1844), p. 308.
26 *Covent Garden Accounts*, British Museum. Egerton MS. 215–218.
27 Hazlitt, XV, 359.
28 *Theatrical Observer*, 15 July, 1822.
29 G. Daniel, Introduction to T. Hook, *Exchange No Robbery, Cumberland's British Theatre* (London, 1829), XXXVII.
30 See: Jim Davis, *"Like Comic Actors on a Stage in Heaven" – Dickens, John Liston and Low Comedy*, in *The Dickensian* (September, 1978) for a fuller consideration of this point.
31 W. Robson, *The Old Playgoer* (London, 1846), p. 118.
32 Scott, *Letters*, IV, 438.
33 M. T. Odell, *Mr. Trotter of Worthing and the Brighton Theatre* (Worthing, 1944), p. 64.
34 Genest, IX, 129–130.
35 *Examiner*, 8 December, 1822.
36 Sir F. Pollock (ed.), *Macready's Reminiscences and Selections from His Diaries and Letters* (London, 1876), p. 210.

37 M. Cowden-Clarke, *My Long Life: An Autobiographical Sketch* (London, 1896), p. 80.

38 *London Magazine* (July, 1822), 186.

39 The circumstances of this performance are recounted in the *Theatrical Observer* 19–20 December, 1822, and in an unidentified clipping, undated, Theatre Cuttings, British Library.

Chapter 5

1 Winston, *Drury Lane Journal*, p. 62.

2 Entry in Charles James Mathews' Manuscript Diary, Princeton University Library

3 *Receipts of Performances*, Vol. VIII (1812–26), British Museum. Add. Ms. 29, 711.

4 Winston, *Drury Lane Journal*, p. 63.

5 Cowden-Clarke, *My Long Life*, p. 80.

6 Winston, *Drury Lane Journal*, p. 69 & p. 138.

7 Manuscript Letter, dated 24 April, 1823, Theatre Museum.

8 *Drama*, New Series I (1825), 72.

9 Crabb Robinson, pp. 102–103.

10 *Theatrical Observer*, 30 September, 1823.

11 Webster, I, 6–7.

12 W. M. Thackeray, *Vanity Fair* (London, 1848), Chapter 48. Thackeray is recalling this particular performance of *The Hypocrite*.

13 P. A. Tasch, *The Dramatic Cobbler: The Life and Works of Isaac Bickerstaffe* (Lewisburg, 1972), p. 176.

14 Mathews, *Memoirs of Charles Mathews, Comedian*, II, 108–111.

15 Genest, IX, 236 & 272.

16 Winston, *Drury Lane Journal*, p. 87.

17 Charles Lamb in *The London Magazine*, July 1824 quoted in George Rowell (ed.), *Victorian Dramatic Criticism* (London, 1971), p. 42.

18 P. Fitzgerald, *Book of Theatrical Anecdotes* (London, 1874), p. 116.

19 *Theatrical Observer*, 4 February, 1829.

20 Manuscript Letter, dated 24 December, 1824, Princeton University Library.

21 A. Bunn, *The Stage Both Before and Behind the Curtain* (London, 1840), I, 62–64.

22 J. W. Cole, *Life and Theatrical Times of Charles Kean* (London, 1859), I, 244.

23 W. Donaldson, *Recollections of an Actor* (London, 1865), p. 162.

24 B. E. Hill, *Playing About and Theatrical Anecdotes and Adventures* (London, 1840), I, 46–51.

25 VII, 433–434. This account is referred to by A. Nicoll, *History of English Drama 1660–1900* (Cambridge, 1952–65), IV, 121.

26 *London Magazine* NSI (January, 1825), 17–22.

27 *Ibid.*, NSI (February, 1825), 231–232.

28 Oxberry, p. 343. The biography of Liston published in *Oxberry's Dramatic Biography and Histrionic Anecdotes*, Vol. I in 1825 was further extended in *Oxberry's Dramatic Mirror*, published in 1828. Basil Francis, in *Fanny Kelly of Drury Lane* (London, 1930), pp. 114–115, writes:

> Let it not be thought that the Oxberry biographies were consistently favourable; they gave praise where praise was justly due but on the other hand they never withheld censure when they considered the subject called for it. It is this blend of light and shade, this impartial analysis of the characters under review that lends an air of verisimilitude to these thumb-nail sketches … Liston (an over-rated actor) is smartly put in his place and his bubble effectively pierced by the Oxberry barb. Liston, with his meritricious acting, "got away with it for years", but the Oxberry's had his measure.

In fact Liston's success to some extent eclipsed Oxberry's career. In the 1820s Oxberry was often called into the Haymarket or Drury Lane merely to make good Liston's absence; his drunkeness and failing memory rendered him too unreliable for long engagements. Consequently, it seems to me that Mr. Francis could not have picked a worse example to testify to the impartiality of the Oxberry biographies.

29 *New Monthly Magazine*, IX (1 March, 1823), 106–107.

Chapter 6

1 *Theatrical Observer*, 1841, quoted in E. B. Watson, *Sheridan to Robertson: A Study of the Nineteenth Century London Stage* (Cambridge, Mass. 1926), p. 63, n. 4.
2 Planché, *Recollections and Reflections*, I, 131–133.
3 J. Poole, *Sketches and Recollections* (London, 1835), p. 408.
4 Genest, IX, 318.
5 *Notes and Queries* Series 8. Vol. II (22 October, 1892), p. 332.
6 *Theatrical Observer*, 5 August, 1826.
7 Webster, I, 7–8.
8 Lady Dorchester (ed.), *Lord Broughton: Recollections of a Long Life* (London, 1907), III, 121.
9 *Theatrical Observer*, 14 November, 1825.
10 *Notes and Queries* Series 8. Vol. II (22 October, 1892), p. 332.
11 *Theatrical Observer*, 15 November, 1825.
12 J. Haslem, *The Old Derby China Factory* (London, 1876), p. 161.
13 M. Dorothy George, *Catalogue of Personal and Political Satires in the British Museum* (London, 1935–54), X, 605.
14 L. Cottrell, *Madame Tussaud* (London, 1951), p. 133.
15 Unidentified Clipping, undated, Liston Clippings, Harvard Theatre Collection.
16 *Liston's Drolleries* (London, 1827), 5th Collection, p. 93.
17 *The Every-Day Book* (10 January, 1826), p. 51.
18 *New York Tribune*, 1 August, 1910.
19 P. Fitzgerald, *A New History of the English Stage* (London, 1882), II, 420.
20 *Athenaeum*, 8 September, 1866.
21 C. & E. Compton (eds.), *Henry Compton: Memoirs* (London, 1879), p. 22.
22 H. Barton Baker, *The London Stage* (London, 1889), I, 197. *Notes and Queries* (Op. cit.) states he was earning £50 a night, but it is more likely that this was his weekly salary, if his fees for other engagements are compared with this.
23 *Paul Pry* was performed at Toole's Theatre with J. L. Toole in the name part from 26/12/1894–9/2/1895. See: J. P. Wearing, *The London Stage 1890–1899: A Calendar of Players and Plays* (New Jersey, 1976), p. 450.

Chapter 7

1 *New Monthly Magazine*, XVIII (February, 1826), 55.
2 Entry in MS. Copy of Winston's Diary for 15 August, 1825. (Not transcribed in Nelson and Cross.)
3 Letterbook of Henry Robertson, Secretary to the Committee of Management of Covent Garden Theatre. British Museum Add. MS. 29643.
4 Manuscript Letter, dated 3 January, 1826, Princeton University Library.
5 *Taunton Courier*, 22 March, 1826.
6 Other partners included Miss Love and Mrs Humby.
7 *Annual Register*, 1846, p. 246.
8 Manuscript Letter, dated 11 December, 1826, Garrick Club Library.
9 *Receipts of Performances*, Vol. VIII (1812–26), British Museum, Add. MS. 29,711.
10 Manuscript Letter, dated 11 February, 1827, Theatre Museum.
11 T. Dibdin, *Reminiscences* (London, 1837), II, 77.
12 Crabb Robinson, p. 120.
13 E. M. Butler, (ed.), *A Regency Visitor – The English Tour of Prince Puckler-Muskau Described in his Letters 1826–1828*, trans. Sarah Austin. (London, 1957), p. 196.
14 *New York Mirror*, 5 March, 1831.
15 Quoted in J. Borgerhoff, *Le Théâtre Anglais à Paris sous la Restauration* (Paris, 1912), p. 74.
16 Hazlitt, XVIII, 160–161.
17 Donaldson, *Recollections of an Actor*, p. 175.
18 Hazlitt, XII, 300.
19 Mathews, *Memoirs of Charles Mathews, Comedian*, III, 638.

20 Entry in MS. Copy of Winston's Diary for 10 March 1827. (Not transcribed in Nelson & Cross).
21 *Theatrical Observer*, 19 December, 1827. A reference to this also occurs in an unpublished manuscript in Manchester City Library – R. J. Broadbent, *Annals of the Manchester Stage*.
22 Genest, IX, 445.
23 *Theatrical Observer*, 10 January, 1828.
24 Mathews, *Memoirs of Charles Mathews, Comedian*, III, 604.
25 *Ibid.*, III, 602.
26 *Ibid.*, III, 634.
27 J. Adolphus, *Memoirs of John Bannister, Comedian* (London, 1839), II, 260.
28 *Athenaeum*, 9 January, 1828.

Chapter 8

1 G. Daniel, Introduction to J. R. Planché, *Charles XII, Cumberland's British Theatre* (London, 1829), XXV.
2 *Ibid.*
3 *Theatrical Observer*, 12 December, 1828.
4 Webster, I, 9.
5 *Theatrical Observer*, 28 July, 1829.
6 *Ibid.*, 24 December, 1828.
7 *Op. cit.*, 7 December, 1828.
8 Planché, *Recollections and Reflections*, I, 180. Planché's statement has been quoted by a number of theatre historians in a context that tends to suggest that Liston was typically representative of old, bad traditions in comic acting. This is partially true, but neglects the nature of Liston's performance in *Charles XII* and his contribution to the Olympic Theatre, which is considered in Chapter 9. In particular, in *Madame Vestris and the London Stage* (New York, 1974), p. 69, William Appleton states that Liston "resented innovation", a somewhat singular interpretation of Planché's remark. Liston's style of acting was arguably quite modern and, at the Olympic, very much within the scope that Vestris demanded. See also: G. Rowell, *The Victorian Theatre* (Oxford, 1967), p. 67 and Nicoll, *A History of English Drama 1660-1900*, IV, 44.
9 *Theatrical Observer*, 1 August, 1829.
10 *Examiner*, 7 November, 1829.
11 G. H. Lewes, *On Actors and the Art of Acting* (London, 1875), pp. 55–56.
12 Manuscript Letter, dated 9 November, Harvard Theatre Collection.
13 W. Marston, *Our Recent Actors* (London, 1888), II, 292–293.
14 Hazlitt, XI, 271.
15 See: Planché, *Recollections and Reflections*, II, 26 and Mathews, *Memoirs of Charles Mathews*, Comedian, III, 638.
16 Manuscript Letter, dated 9 November, Harvard Theatre Collection. The date is incomplete but the reference to Fanny Kemble indicates it was written in 1829.
17 R. B. Peake, Preface to *Master's Rival, Cumberland's British Theatre*, (London, 1829), XXII.
18 Winston, *Drury Lane Journal*, 147. See also: *Theatrical Observer*, 16 May, 1827.
19 Quoted in E. & E. Johnson (eds.), *The Dickens Theatrical Reader* (London, 1964), pp. 48–49.
20 Manuscript Letter, dated 14 January, 1829, Harvard Theatre Collection.
21 *Dramatic Magazine*, June, 1830.
22 *Theatrical Observer*, 27 May, 1830.

Chapter 9

1 *Examiner*, 9 October, 1831.
2 Planché, *Recollections and Reflections*, I, 183.
3 Appleton, *Madame Vestris and the London Stage*, p. 65.
4 J. M. Langford, "Some Olympic Reminiscences", *The Era Almanack* (London, 1870), p. 72.
5 Webster, I, 7. Webster was a member of the Olympic Company at this time.

6 W. Burke Wood, *Personal Recollections of the Stage* (Philadelphia, 1855), p. 329. According to *The British Stage or Dramatic Censor* I (May, 1831), no. 2 p. 72 Liston gave Emma a marriage portion of £10,000.

7 *Notes and Queries*, Series 8. Vol. III (1 April, 1893).

8 *Illustrated London News* VIII (March, 1846), 246.

9 Manuscript Note in Liston's handwriting, Harvard Theatre Collection.

10 Manuscript Letter, dated 19 August, 1831, New York Public Library.

11 *Op. cit.*, 21 March, 1832.

12 Unidentified clipping, undated, Olympic Theatre Cuttings, British Library.

13 See: E. Costigan "Drama and Everyday Life in *Sketches by Boz*" in *R.E.S.* New Series, Vol. XXVII, No. 108 (1976).

14 Crabb Robinson, p. 138.

15 Macready, *Reminiscences*, p. 292.

16 Unidentified clipping, dated 25 January, 1833, Liston Clippings, Harvard Theatre Collection.

17 *Theatrical Observer*, 12 January, 1833.

18 Unidentified clipping, undated, Liston Clippings, Harvard Theatre Collection.

19 Manuscript Letter, dated 14 January, 1833, Theatre Museum.

20 Unidentified clipping, dated 27 January, 1833, Olympic Theatre Cuttings, British Library.

21 *Ibid.*, undated.

22 *Theatrical Observer*, 12 July, 1832.

23 Bunn, *The Stage, Both Before and Behind the Curtain*, I, 181–182.

24 *Ibid.*, p. 182.

25 *Hush Money* was by George Dance, *Fighting By Proxy* by James Kenney. Keeley was even more restrained than Liston in performance. In the 1820s the *Athenaeum* predicted that he would eventually be as great a favourite as Liston. The dramatist Edward Fitzball wrote in 1859 that, even in Liston's day, he preferred Keeley to Liston in some points. See: E. Fitzball, *Thirty Five Years of a Dramatic Author's Life* (London, 1859), I, 102.

26 *The Retort Courteous* is not among the manuscript plays submitted to the Lord Chamberlain during 1834. Consequently, the details of the play are pieced together from reviews.

27 Langford, *Some Olympic Reminiscences*, p. 73.

28 Marston, *Our Recent Actors*, II, 160.

29 Manuscript Letter, dated 13 September, 1836, New York Public Library.

30 Unidentified clipping, dated 7 December, 1836. Olympic Theatre Cuttings. British Library.

31 Crabb Robinson, p. 154.

32 Langford, *Some Olympic Reminiscences*, p. 73.

33 *Theatrical Observer*, 18–31 May, 1837.

34 Unidentified clipping, dated 2 June, 1837, Olympic Theatre Cuttings, British Library.

35 Liston's six years at the Olympic have not really been given the attention they deserve. Many accounts of his engagement under Vestris are marred by inaccuracy. Matthew Mackintosh, a Scots carpenter employed at the Olympic, is totally inaccurate, when he writes in his *Stage Reminiscences ... by an old stager* (Glasgow, 1866), p. 69 that Liston was the first to give his support when Vestris took over the Olympic. He was still at Drury Lane when Vestris took on the Olympic and only joined her once the success of the venture seemed proven. C. E. Pearce in *Madame Vestris and Her Times* (London, 1923), pp. 165 & 217 states Liston did not appear at the Olympic until 1834 and that he retired in January 1836. Clifford Williams in *Madame Vestris: A Theatrical Biography* (London, 1973), p. 95 writes that "most of the cast of *Paul Pry* were in the first Olympic season, including Liston himself, Madame's trump card among the gentlemen". He adds (p. 106) that *The Little Jockey* was the play selected for Liston's debut, but an examination of Olympic playbills reveals that Liston never performed in this play. Most contentious is W. Appleton in *Madame Vestris and the London Stage*. He suggests that Liston was more and more out of place at the Olympic as Vestris's productions "moved increasingly in the direction of naturalism" (p. 69) and that the spectators attracted by Liston were not the sort of clientele Vestris wished to have at her theatre (pp. 69–70). In fact, Liston's style of acting probably harmonised with Vestris's intentions, as the many favourable reviews of Liston at the Olympic testify. Also, rather than attract undesirables, his engagement helped to keep the theatre full. Appleton adds (p. 70) "No doubt Liston was aware of her feelings. His performances were often slipshod and he is said to have sometimes 'reeled through' them." Appleton is basing this statement on the failure of *The Young Hopefuls*, which is in no way typical of Liston's performance at the Olympic. Appleton also implies that

the removal of the gallery, to be replaced by a second tier of boxes, was aided by the imminent retirement of Liston and that the engagement of Charles Mathews was drawing an increasingly fashionable audience and ousting the Liston supporters (p. 100). In fact, it is unlikely that Vestris was glad to see the back either of Liston or his supporters and, in plays such as *The Two Figaros* and *The Old and Young Stager*, she was glad to combine the contrasting yet complimentary style of the two actors. Appleton then states (p. 101):

> The 1836–37 season opened with Planché's *Court Favour* ... The play was entirely a vehicle for Liston, providing him with a series of broad jokes based on that inexhaustible source of humour, his "inexpressibles" or breeches. A year earlier audiences had roared at the same jokes in Samuel Lover's *The Beau Ideal*. Madame was perhaps a trifle put out to find that despite the disappearance of the gallery, the laughter, at least when Liston was on stage, was as loud as ever. But if audiences relished their old favourite as much as before, they were also capable of appreciating the subtler comic style of Mathews.

The views expressed here are most surprising, for a number of reasons, not least of which is the fact that Liston did not appear in *Court Favour*. Why should Madame Vestris be "put out" to find that audiences still laughed at Liston? Wasn't that why she employed him? Nor is it strange that Charles Mathews, a light comedian, should seem more subtle than Liston, a low comedian. This would normally have been the case. Appleton himself refers to the influence of the elder Mathews, with whom Liston worked so well, on his son (p. 101). Although Appleton's biography is generally the most accurate, scholarly and readable of the different lives of Vestris published during this century, his interpretation of Liston's role within the Olympic company fails to take account of the accumulation of evidence that suggests that Liston, far from being out of place, was a crucial figure in the Olympic's history and had mastered a style of acting totally appropriate to Vestris's intentions.

Chapter 10

1 *Actors by Daylight*, No. 14 (2 June, 1838), 110.
2 Macready, *Reminiscences*, p. 424.
3 Bunn, *The Stage, Both Before and Behind the Curtain*, II, 282.
4 Macready, *Reminiscences*, p. 433.
5 *Ibid.*, pp. 455 & 479.
6 C. Dickens Jr. (ed.), *The Life of Charles James Mathews: chiefly autobiographical* (London, 1879), II, pp. 88–89.
7 *Ibid.*
8 Planché, *Recollections and Reflections*, II, 26.
9 H. Barton Baker, *Our Old Actors* (London, 1878), II, 314.
10 Fitzball, *Thirty Five Years of a Dramatic Author's Life*, pp. 306–307.
11 The *Theatrical Journal*, 31 July, 1841, states that Liston's daughter appeared in the provinces as a singer with the actor Yates and his wife, although there is no further evidence to substantiate this. A performer named Miss Land is referred to several times as the niece of Liston in the *Theatrical Journal*. A playbill for the Richmond Theatre, 22 October, 1828, in the author's collection, states that Liston "has kindly offered his services" for the occasion of Miss Land's benefit, but no family connection is mentioned.
12 Webster, I, 6.
13 *Era*, 25 November, 1838.
14 Planché, *Recollections and Reflections*, II, 26.
15 Dramatic Biography Theatre Cuttings, British Library.
16 *Illustrated London News*, VIII (28 March, 1846), 214.
17 Dramatic Biography Theatre Cuttings, British Library.
18 *Gentleman's Magazine*, 1846, p. 660.
19 *Ibid.*, p. 547.
20 The marriage of Liston's elder grand-daughter, Emma, is recorded in the *Annual Register* Vol. XLV (Jan.–June, 1856): At Metfield, Suffolk, Evelyn Philip *Meadows* Esq., Captain Royal Essex Rifles, son

of the late D. R. Meadows Esq., of Burghesh House, Suffolk to Emma, elder daughter of the late G. H. Rodwell.

21 *Some Recollections of Liston* from *Hood's Magazine*, Forster Collection, Victoria and Albert Museum.

Chapter 11

1 *Mirror of the Stage*, II (10 February, 1823), 25.
2 Unidentified clipping, undated. Olympic Theatre Cuttings, British Library.
3 *Ibid.*
4 R. Findlater in *Joe Grimaldi: His Life and Theatre*, 2nd edition (Cambridge, 1978) pp. 156–157 discusses the use of make-up by Munden and Grimaldi.
5 *Op. cit.*, 5 March, 1831.
6 *Drama*, V (October, 1823), 88.
7 *Mirror of the Stage*, III (8 September, 1823), 41–42.
8 *New Monthly Magazine*, IX (1 October, 1823), 74.
9 *London Magazine*, VIII (September, 1823), 321.
10 *Theatrical Observer*, 2 May, 1823.
11 G. Daniel, Introduction to I. Bickerstaffe, *The Hypocrite, Cumberland's British Theatre*, III.
12 *Theatrical Observer*, 14 May, 1824.
13 Quoted in Rowell, *Victorian Dramatic Criticism*, p. 39.
14 *New York Mirror*, 5 March, 1831.
15 *News*, 19 July, 1807.
16 J. E. Morpurgo (ed.), *The Autobiography of Leigh Hunt* (London, 1948), p. 186.
17 *Ibid.*
18 Hazlitt, XVIII, 352.
19 Hunt, *Autobiography*, p. 132.
20 *New York Mirror*, 5 March, 1831.
21 Marston, *Our Recent Actors*, II, 292.
22 Hunt, *Autobiography*, 132.
23 *Brighton Gazette*, 2 March, 1826.
24 *Liverpool Theatrical Investigator*, II (9 November, 1822), 279.
25 *London Magazine*, VIII (October, 1823), 433.
26 Webster, I, 9.
27 *Op. cit.*, V (January, 1824), 261.
28 *Op. cit.*, VI (July, 1822), 186.
29 G. Daniel, Introduction to T. Hook, *Catch Him Who Can, Cumberland's British Theatre* (London, 1829), XL.
30 *Op. cit.*, 14 September, 1829.
31 *Op. cit.*, 5 March, 1832.
32 Hill, *Playing About*, I, 196.
33 *Op. cit.*, 16 June, 1805.
34 Marston, *Our Recent Actors*, II, 160.
35 *Op. cit.*, 5 March, 1831.
36 Daniel, Introduction to *Catch Him Who Can, Cumberland's British Theatre*.
37 T. Hook, *Sayings and Doings* (London, 1825), II, 64.
38 Hazlitt, XVIII, 196.
39 Hill, *Playing About*, I, 294.
40 Hazlitt, V, 192.
41 *Brighton Gazette*, 13 January, 1825.
42 *Ibid.*
43 Marston, *Our Recent Actors*, II, 292.
44 G. Daniel, Introduction to W. Congreve, *Love for Love, Cumberland's British Theatre* (London, 1829), XIX.
45 G. Daniel, Introduction to R. Cumberland, *The Wheel of Fortune, Cumberland's British Theatre* (London, 1829), XIV.
46 *Op. cit.*, IV (8 March, 1824), 35.

47 *Theatrical Observer*, 10 January, 1828.

48 *Op. cit.*, 16 November, 1825.

49 G. Daniel, *Memoir of Mr. Harley*, prefaced to G. Colman. *The Heir at Law, Cumberland's British Theatre*.

50 *New York Mirror*, 5 March, 1831.

51 Lord William Pitt Lennox, *Plays, Players and Playhouses at Home and Abroad* (London, 1881), I, 252.

52 *Mirror of the Stage*, IV (24 May, 1824), 93.

53 J. Boaden, *Life of Mrs Jordan* (London, 1831), 198.

54 *Theatrical Observer*, 3 January, 1826.

55 G. Wightwick, *Theatricals Forty Five Years Ago* (Portishead, 1862), p. 13.

56 Webster, I, 9.

57 *Op. cit.*, VIII (28 March, 1846), 214.

58 *Authentic Memoirs of the Green-Room* (London, 1806), IV, 41.

59 James Boaden quoted in W. Clark Russell, *Representative Actors* (London and New York, 1888), pp. 323–324.

60 Unidentified clipping, dated Dublin 26 November, Theatre Cuttings 61, British Library.

61 *Edinburgh Evening Courant*, 5 April, 1817.

62 *Authentic Memoirs of the Green-Room* (London, 1806), IV, 41.

63 *Op. cit.*, NSI (1825), 72.

64 *Examiner*, 4 June, 1837. However, in discussing the use of the word "natural" in relation to nineteenth century acting, one has to bear in mind the multiplicity of meanings inherent in the term. The O.E.D. defines "natural" in relation to acting as "having the ease or simplicity of nature; free from affectation, artificiality or constraint; simple, unaffected, easy". Liston, of course, played characters who were highly affected and, in the writing, often exaggerated. Yet he managed to make them credible, as Leigh Hunt testified in *Critical Essays*. For useful discussions of the term "natural" see: Lewes, *On Actors and the Art of Acting*, pp. 14–125 and Eric Bentley, *The Dramatic Event* (Boston, Mass., 1954), p. 80.

65 Boaden, *Life of Mrs Jordan*, II, 198.

66 Cole, *The Life and Times of Charles Kean*, I, 243.

67 *Theatrical Looker-On*, 4 November, 1822.

68 *Bristol Gazette*, 19 February, 1824.

69 Quoted in Clark Russell, *Representative Actors*, pp. 323–324.

70 *Op. cit.*, V (January, 1824), 261.

71 Hazlitt, XVIII, 403.

72 Boaden, *Life of Mrs Jordan*, II, 198.

73 Hazlitt, XVIII, 359.

74 Clipping, undated, from the *Spectator*, Dramatic Biography Theatre Cuttings, British Library.

75 Watson, *Sheridan to Robertson*, p. 315.

Bibliography

Books

Adolphus, John, *Memoirs of John Bannister, Comedian*. London 1838.

Album of the Cambridge Garrick Club, Cambridge 1836,

Appleton, William, *Madame Vestris and the London Stage*. New York 1974.

Archer, William, *The Old Drama and the New*. London 1933.

Authentic Memoirs of the Green-Room, 4 vols. London 1806.

—— London 1814(?)

Clinton-Baddeley, V. C., *The Burlesque Tradition in the English Theatre after 1600*. London 1952.

Barton-Baker, H., *A History of the London Stage*. London 1904

—— *Our Old Actors*. London 1878.

Barham, R. H., *Life and Remains of T. E. Hook*. London 1853.

Barker, Kathleen M. D., *The Theatre Royal Bristol. Two Centuries of Stage History*. London 1974.

Barrow, William, *An Essay on Education*. Second edition. 2 vols. London 1804.

Baynham, W., *The Glasgow Stage*. Glasgow 1892.

Boaden, James, *The Life of Mrs. Jordan*. 2 vols. London 1831.

—— *Memoirs of the Life of John Philip Kemble*. 2 vols. London 1825.

—— *Memoirs of Mrs. Siddons*. 2 vols. London 1827.

Booth, Michael, *English Melodrama*. London 1965.

—— (ed.), *English Plays of the Nineteenth Century*. 5 vols. Oxford 1965–76.

Borgerhoff, J., *Le Théâtre Anglais a Parais sous Le Restauration*. Paris 1912.

Broadbent, R. J., *Annals of the Liverpool Stage*. Liverpool 1901.

Buckstone, G. B. (ed.), *Broad Grins*. London 1872.

Bunn, Alfred, *The Stage, Both Before and Behind the Curtain*. 3 vols. London 1840.

Burke Wood. W., *Personal Recollections of the Stage*. Philadelphia 1855.

Chaulin, N. P., *Biographie Dramatique des principaux artistes anglais venus à Paris, précedée de Souvenirs historique du théâtre anglais en 1827 et 1828*. Paris 1828.

Clare, Martin and Barwis, Cuthbert, *Rules and Orders for the Government of the Academy in Soho-Square, London*. London 1740.

Cole, J. W., *Life and Theatrical Times of Charles Kean.* 2 vols. London 1859.

Colman, George the younger, *Random Records.* 2 vols. London 1830.

Compton, Henry, *Henry Compton: Memoirs.* ed. C. & E. Compton. London 1879.

Cotton, William, *The Story of the Drama in Exeter.* Exeter 1887.

Cottrell, L., *Madame Tussaud.* London 1951.

Cowden-Clarke, Mary, *My Long Life: An Autobiographical Sketch.* London 1896.

Cruse, A., *The Englishman and his Books in the early Nineteenth Century.* London 1930.

Daniel, George (ed.), *Cumberland's British Theatre.* 48 vols. London 1829.

Dibdin, J. C., *The Annals of the Edinburgh Stage.* Edinburgh 1888.

Dibdin, Thomas J., *Reminiscences.* 2 vols. London 1837.

Dictionary of National Biography

Donaldson, Walter, *Recollections of an Actor.* London 1865.

Donohue, Joseph W., *Theatre in the Age of Kean.* Oxford 1975.

— — (ed.), *The Theatrical Manager in England and America.* Princeton 1971.

Doran, John & R. W. Lowe, *Their Majesties Servants.* 3 vols. London 1888.

Dorchester, Lady (ed.), *Edward Lord Broughton. Recollections of a Long Life.* 6 vols. London 1907.

Downer, Alan S., *The Eminent Tragedian William Charles Macready.* Cambridge, Mass. 1966.

Duncombe, Thomas, *Life and Correspondence of T. S. Duncombe.* 2 vols. London 1868.

Findlater, Richard, *Joe Grimaldi His Life and Theatre.* Second edition. Cambridge 1978.

Fitzball, Edward, *Thirty Five Years of a Dramatic Author's Life.* London 1859.

Fitzgerald, Percy, *Book of Theatrical Anecdotes.* London 1874.

— — *A New History of the English Stage.* 2 vols. London 1882.

Foote, Horace, *A Companion to the Theatres.* London 1829.

Francis, Basil, *Fanny Kelly of Drury Lane.* London 1950.

Genest, John, *Some Account of the English Stage.* 10 vols. Bath 1832.

George, M. Dorothy, *Catalogue of Personal and Political Satires.* vols. VIII–X. London 1935–54.

The Georgian Playhouse Catalogue. London 1975.

Gilliland, Thomas, *The Dramatic Mirror.* London 1808.

Hall, John, *Staffordshire Portrait Figures.* London 1973.

Hare, Arnold, *The Georgian Theatre in Wessex.* London 1958.

Haslem, Joseph, *The Old Derby China Factory.* London 1876.

Hazlitt, William, *Complete Works*, ed. P. P. Howe. 21 vols. London 1930–34.

Hill, Benson Earl, *Playing About and Theatrical Anecdotes and Adventures.* 2 vols. London 1840.

History of the Theatre Royal Dublin, Dublin 1870.

Hogan, Charles Beecher, *The London Stage, 1660–1800 Part V: 1776–1800.* S. Illinois 1968.

Holman, L. E., *Lamb's "Barbara S-".* London 1925.

Hook, Theodore, *Choice Humorous Works*. London 1873.

— — *Gilbert Gurney*. London 1836.

— — *Sayings and Doings*. 2nd Series. London 1825.

Hunt, Leigh, *The Autobiogaphy of Leigh Hunt*, ed. J. E. Morpurgo. London 1948.

— — *Critical Essays on the Performers of the London Theatres*. London 1807.

— — *Leigh Hunt's Dramatic Criticism*, ed. L. H. & C. W. Houtchens. New York 1949.

Kelly, Michael, *Reminiscences*, ed. T. E. Hook. 2 vols. London 1826.

Kemble, Fanny, *Records of a Girlhood*. 2 vols. New York 1879.

King, Robert, *North Shields Theatres*. Gateshead on Tyne 1948.

Lamb, Charles, *Lamb's Dramatic Essays*, ed. Brander Matthews. London 1891.

— — *The Letters of Charles Lamb*, ed. Alfred Ainger. 2 vols. London 1888.

— — *The Letters of Charles and Mary Lamb*, ed. Edwin W. Marrs Jnr. London and Ithaca 1978.

Larwood, Jacob, *Theatrical Anecdotes*. London 1882.

Leathers, Victor, *British Entertainers in France*. Toronto 1959.

Lee, Henry, *Memoirs of a Manager*. Taunton 1830.

Leech, Clifford & T. W. Craik (eds.), *The Revels History of Drama in English vol. VI 1750–1880*. London 1975.

Lennox, Lord William Pitt, *Celebrities I have Known*. London 1876.

— — *Plays, Players and Playhouses at Home and Abroad*. 2 vols. London 1881.

Leslie, R. C., *Autobiographical Recollections*. 2 vols. London 1886.

Levey, R. M. & J. O. O'Rourke, *Annals of the Theatre Royal, Dublin*. Dublin 1880.

Lewes, G. H., *On Actors and the Art of Acting*. London 1875.

Liston's Drolleries, Collections Third and Fifth. London 1827.

Mackintosh, Matthew, *Stage Reminiscences ... by an old stager*. Glasgow 1866.

Macready, William Charles, *Macready's Reminiscences and Selections from his Diaries and Letters*, ed. Sir Frederick Pollock. London 1876.

Mander, Raymond & Joe Mitchenson, *The Lost Theatres of London*. London 1968.

Marston, Westland, *Our Recent Actors*. 2 vols. London 1888.

Mathews, Ann, *Anecdotes of Actors*. London 1844.

— — *Memoirs of Charles Mathews, Comedian*. 4 vols. London 1838–39.

— — *Tea-Table Talk*. 2 vols. London 1857.

Memoirs of the public and private life, adventures and wonderful exploits of Madame Vestris. London c.a. 1830.

Maude, Cyril, *The Haymarket Some Records and Reminiscences*. London 1903.

Mayer, David III, *Harlequin in his Element – The English Pantomime 1806–1836*. Cambridge, Mass. 1969.

Munden, Thomas S., *Memoirs of Joseph Shepherd Munden, Comedian*. London 1846.

Murray, Christopher, *Robert William Elliston Manager. A Theatrical Biography*. London 1975.

Nelson, Alfred L. & B. Gilbert Cross, eds., *Drury Lane Journal – Selections from James Winston's Diaries 1819–1827*. London 1974.

The Newcastle Jester. Newcastle 1804.

Nicoll, Allardyce, *A History of English Drama 1660–1900*. 6 vols. Cambridge 1952–1965.

Odell, George C., *Shakespeare from Betterton to Irving*. 2 vols. New York 1920.

Odell, M. T., *Mr. Trotter of Worthing and the Brighton Theatre*. Aylesbury 1944.

—— *The Old Theatre Worthing*. Aylesbury 1938.

Oswald, H., *The Theatre Royal in Newcastle Upon Tyne*. Newcastle 1936.

Oulton, W. C., *A History of the Theatres in London*. 3 vols. London 1818.

Oxberry, William, *Dramatic Biography and Histrionic Anecdotes*. 5 vols. London 1825–26.

—— *Oxberry's Dramatic Mirror*. London 1828.

Peake, R. B., *Memoirs of the Colman Family*. 2 vols. London 1841.

Pearce, Charles E., *Madame Vestris and Her Times*. London 1923.

Penley, Belville S., *The Bath Stage*. London 1892.

Planché, James Robinson, *Extravaganzas*. London 1879.

—— *Recollections and Reflections*. 2 vols. London 1872.

Poole, John, *Sketches and Recollections*. London 1835.

Pope, W. MacQueen, *Haymarket Theatre of Perfection*. London 1948.

Porter, H., *History of the Theatres of Brighton*. Brighton 1886.

Puckler-Muskau, Hermann, *A Regency Visitor – The English Tour of Prince Puckler-Muskau Described in his letters 1826–1828*, trans. Sarah Austin, ed. E. M. Butler. London 1957.

Raymond, George, *The Life and Enterprises of Robert William Elliston, Comedian*. London 1857.

—— *Memoirs of Robert William Elliston, Comedian*. 2 vols. London 1844–45.

Reynolds, Frederick, *The Life and Times of Frederick Reynolds*. 2 vols. London 1826.

Rice, D. G., *The Illustrated Guide to Rockingham Pottery and Porcelain*. London 1971.

—— *Rockingham Ornamental Porcelain*. London 1966.

Richards, Kenneth & Peter Thomson (eds.), *The Eighteenth Century English Stage*. London 1972.

—— *Nineteenth Century British Theatre*. London 1971.

Richardson Joanna, *George IV A Portrait*. London 1966.

Robinson, Henry Crabb, *Diaries, Reminiscences and Correspondence of Henry Crabb Robinson*, ed. T. Sadler. London 1869.

—— *The London Theatre 1811–1866. Selections from the Diary of Henry Crabb Robinson*, ed. Eluned Brown. London 1966.

Robson, William, *The Old Playgoer*. London 1846.

Rosenthal, Harold, *Two Centuries of Opera at Covent Garden*. London 1958.

Rowell, George, *The Victorian Theatre*. Revised edition. Oxford 1967.

—— (ed.), *Victorian Dramatic Criticism*. London 1971.

Russell, W. Clark, *Representative Actors*. London and New York 1888.

Ryan, Richard, *Dramatic Table Talk*. London 1825.

Scott, Sir Walter, *The Letters of Sir Walter Scott*, ed. H. Grierson. 12 vols. London 1932–37.

Shore, W. Teignmouth, *D'Orsay; or the Complete Dandy*. London 1911.

Sprague, A. C., *Shakespeare and the Actors*. Cambridge, Mass. 1944.

Stirling, E., *Old Drury Lane. Fifty Years Recollections of Author, Actor and Manager*. 2 vols. London 1881.

Stockdale, J. J., *Covent Garden Journal*. London 1810.

Stockwell, La Tourette, *Dublin Theatres and Theatre Customs 1637–1820*. Kingsport Tennessee 1938.

Survey of London, gen. ed. F. H. W. Sheppard. Vol. XXXIII. London 1966.

Thackeray, William Makepeace, *Vanity Fair*. London 1848.

— — *William Makepeace Thackeray. Letters and Private Papers*. ed. G. N. Ray. Cambridge, Mass. 1940.

Toole, J. L., *Reminiscences of J. L. Toole*, ed. J. Hatton. London 1889.

Tasch, Peter A., *The Dramatic Cobbler: The Life and Works of Isaac Bickerstaffe*. Lewisburg 1972.

Trewin, J. C., *The Night Has Been Unruly*. London 1937.

Troubridge, Sir St. Vincent, *The Benefit System in the British Theatre*. London 1967.

Trussler, Simon (ed.), *Burlesque Plays of the Eighteenth Century*. Oxford 1969.

Waitzkin, Leo, *The Witch of Wych Street*. Cambridge, Mass. 1933.

Watson, Ernest Bradlee, *Sheridan to Robertson. A Study of the Nineteenth Century Drama*. Cambridge, Mass. 1926.

Webster's Acting National Drama. London 1937.

White, Henry A., *Sir Walter Scott's Novels on the Stage*. New Haven 1927.

Whyte, Frederic, *Actors of the Century*. London 1898.

Wightwick, George, *Theatre Forty Five Years Ago*. Portishead 1862.

Williams, Clifford John, *Madame Vestris. A Theatrical Biography*. London 1973.

Williamson J., *Charles Kemble, Man of the Theatre*. Lincoln, Nebr. 1970.

Winston, James, *Theatric Tourist*. London 1805.

Wyndham, Henry Saxe-, *Annals of Covent Garden Theatre*. London 1905.

Yates, E., *Fifty Years of London Life*. London 1885.

Newspapers and Periodicals

Actors by Daylight

Actors by Gaslight

The Age

The Annual Register

The Athenaeum

Le Beau Monde

The Brighton Gazette

The Bristol Gazette

The British Stage and Literary Cabinet

The Censor

The Champion

The Court Journal

The Daily Advertiser

The Drama or Theatrical Pocket Magazine

The Dramatic Magazine
Dramatic Memoirs and Criticisms
Edinburgh Evening Courant
The Era
Era Almanack
European Magazine
The Examiner
The Exeter Flying Post
Figaro in London
Gentleman's Magazine
Hampshire Telegraph and Sussex Chronicle
Hood's Magazine
The Illustrated London News
John Bull
Journal Des Debats
The Liverpool Mercury
The Liverpool Theatrical Investigator
The Manchester Guardian
The Mirror of the Stage
The Monthly Mirror
The Monthly Theatrical Reporter
The Morning Chronicle
The Morning Herald
The New Monthly Magazine

The Newcastle Advertiser
The Newcastle Chronicle
The News
The New York Mirror
Nineteenth Century Theatre Research
Notes and Queries
The Opera Glass
The Quarterly Review
The Stage
The Statesman
The Sun
The Tatler
The Taunton Courier
Theatre Notebook
The Theatrical Inquisitor
The Theatrical Looker-On
*The Theatrical Observer and Daily Bills
  of the Play*
The Times
The Theatrical Journal
The Tyne Mercury
Walker's Hibernian Magazine
The York Courant
The York Herald

Playbills
The following playbill collections have been used:

British Library
Adelphi Theatre
Bath
Birmingham
Covent Garden
Drury Lane
Edinburgh
Glasgow
Haymarket Theatre
Liverpool
Lyceum Theatre
Newcastle
Olympic Theatre

Harvard Theatre Collection
Dublin
Weymouth

Newcastle Public Library
Newcastle

Royal Irish Academy
Dublin

Somerset County Records Office
Taunton

Theatre Museum
Covent Garden
Drury Lane
Haymarket
Olympic

Theatre Cuttings
The following collections of theatre cuttings have been used:

British Library
Dramatic Biography Theatre Cuttings
Drury Lane Theatre Cuttings
Lyceum Theatre Cuttings
Olympic Theatre Cuttings
Theatre Cuttings 61
Winston, James, *A Collection of Memoranda,*
   Documents, Playbills, Newspapers etc., from
   1616–1830

Harvard Theatre Collection
John Liston Clippings
Paul Pry Clippings

New York Public Library
Liston Clippings

Theatre Museum
Haymarket Theatre
Olympic Theatre

Manuscripts
Manuscript letters, receipts, account books, plays have been examined from the
   following collections:

British Library
Covent Garden Account Books. Egerton MSS. 2303–2323
Letterbook of Henry Robertson, Secretary to the Committee of Management of Covent Garden
   Theatre – Add. MS. 29643.

Plays Submitted to the Lord Chamberlain 1824–1851
Receipts of Performances. Add MS. 29,711.

Harvard Theatre Collection
Letters

New York Public Library
Letters

Princeton University Library
Diaries and Manuscript Letters – Mathews Papers.

Theatre Museum
Letters
Microfilm of Winston's Diary

Other Sources:
Garrick Club Library, Shakespeare Birthday Trust
Huntington Library, Westervelt Collection, Columbia University

Index